The Curious Gardeners

Obsession and Diversity in
45 British Gardens

GUY COOPER and **GORDON TAYLOR**

Photographs by Clive Boursnell

HEADLINE

First published in 2001 by
HEADLINE BOOK PUBLISHING

By arrangement with the BBC

The BBC logo and the 'Curious Gardeners' logo are trade
marks of the British Broadcasting Corporation and are used
under licence

BBC logo © BBC 1996
'The Curious Gardeners' logo © BBC 2000

Guy Cooper and Gordon Taylor would be happy to hear
from readers with their comments on the book at the
following e-mail address: g.taylor@clara.net

10 9 8 7 6 5 4 3 2 1

British Library Cataloguing in Publication Data:

Cooper, Guy, 1934–
    The curious gardeners
    1. Gardens – Great Britain – Design
    I. Title II. Taylor, Gordon, 1935 –
    712.6'0941

    ISBN 0 7472 3614 3

Designed by Andrew Barron & Collis Clements Associates
Edited by Helena Attlee
Printed and bound in Great Britain by Butler & Tanner Ltd,
Frome and London

HEADLINE BOOK PUBLISHING
A division of Hodder Headline
338 Euston Road, London NW1 3BH

www.headline.co.uk
www.hodderheadline.com

Also by Guy Cooper and Gordon Taylor

English Herb Gardens

English Water Gardens

Paradise Transformed:
The Private Garden for the Twenty-First Century

Gardens of Obsession:
Eccentric and Extravagant Visions

Gardens for the Future:
Gestures Against the Wild

Mirrors of Paradise:
The Gardens of Fernando Caruncho

ACKNOWLEDGEMENTS

Our thanks to Clive Boursnell for his meticulous skill which has produced the superb images of the gardens.

Myriad and especial thanks to Heather Holden-Brown and Celia Kent and to all of their highly energetic and first-rate team at Headline. The largest ongoing thanks as always, which need not be listed here, to our friend and agent, Patricia White of Rogers, Coleridge and White, and her sorcerer's apprentice and leading cyberchick, Rebecca Price.

On the television series, a high salute of gratitude to Tim Richardson, gardens writer for *Country Life* and brilliant founder-editor of *New Eden: The Contemporary Gardens Magazine*, an extremely exciting, worthwhile and unique venture which, alas, was closed after only 12 months' existence. He put our names forward to BBC Bristol, for which we must thank him always.

Massive thanks to Jane Root, Controller of BBC2, for commissioning the six half-hour series 'The Curious Gardeners', on which this book is based.

A further salute to BBC Bristol and all of the personnel with whom we worked or who were involved in the realisation of the series. The unit produced imaginative and efficient work of the highest quality to achieve the series. Multiple thanks to Ian James Pye, the first director from BBC Bristol with whom we worked. To Jeremy Gibson, who most of all had the vision to express his opinion forcefully that we were knowledgeable and eccentric garden designers who can communicate and that the series must be done. To Mark Hill, Executive Producer extraordinary, and his assistant, Lynda Griffiths. To Ben Southwell, Series Producer and a Director of three episodes, who was always intelligent and cool in any situation, and 'the boy with the toy' for choosing the beloved Alvis drop-head coupé, the Curious Gardeners' transport for the series. To Red Triangle for finding the car and Sean Costello for letting us use it. To Patty Kraus for all her imaginative hard work as Director of the other three episodes, as well as those superb cameramen, John Couzens and Paul Hutchins, and the ever-patient sound man, Gordon Nightingale. To the brilliant researchers for finding the highly contrasted basis of the series, the *gardens*, with thanks to both Claire Markwell and Patsy Titcomb; Holly Chester, PA, and the Production Manager, Sophie Cole, of the punk hair and the abacus for the series' budget and matters financial.

To all the garden owners and others on whatever level of obsession at the almost fifty garden sites we explored and filmed in Devon and Cornwall, Yorkshire, Gloucestershire, Herefordshire and Worcestershire, Buckinghamshire, Norfolk and Scotland, where there was such cooperation and a wonderful welcome, only to be described as the very Best of British.

TO ANNE M.W. MANSON

Contents

GARDENS ECCENTRIC

GARDENS CONTEMPORARY

Introduction

This hedged circle (opposite), on the garden side of Kerscott, directs the eye out to a main axis and other focal points, many of which are site-generated, the late twentieth-century improvement on Alexander Pope's great garden design admonition, 'consult the genius of the place'.

Take an Englishman, with no Scots, Welsh or Irish blood in him, and an American who has lived in Britain for the last thirty-four years. Provide a 1960s Alvis coupé for them to drive, a camera crew and a list of gardens to visit. These were the ingredients that went into the making of BBC Bristol's *The Curious Gardeners* television series.

Our philosophy of landscape design has developed over a period of about eighteen years. Being self-taught, we had to read widely and take ourselves off to lectures whenever we could. In short, we've done as much 'homework' as possible. We were inspired by a desire to accumulate knowledge quickly and to achieve an in-depth understanding of the different approaches to design. This knowledge was to be used as a tool that would enable us to design gardens in any style we chose. This is not as pompous as it sounds. We have always been confident in our ability because, quite early on, we found ourselves obsessed by gardens and landscapes of all periods. This obsessive relationship with the subject is the key to success. Since most of our work has been for private clients, we have designed gardens and landscapes to surround houses of many different architectural styles, including medieval, Elizabethan, Carolean, Georgian and Arts and Crafts. One of our largest and most traditionally British projects was the design master plan and installation of the gardens for Sir Elton John's 14-hectare (36-acre) estate at Old Windsor. At the other end of the spectrum was a small-scale and very contemporary design for a Russian tycoon. Laid out on his two penthouse terraces overlooking the Thames, it included Astroturf, silvered-concrete reinforcing mesh and a fountain of copper wire and Perspex. This design was completed in 1999. It was one of a number of sites that mark a steadily increasing demand for contemporary gardens, reflecting the style of the late twentieth and early twenty-first centuries.

Early on in our home-made course on design, we came up against Alexander Pope, that eighteenth-century luminary. His advice to would-be designers was to 'consult the Genius of the Place in all'. This became our motto, our guiding principle. We believe that the twentieth-century site-generated approach represents a contemporary realisation of Pope's theory of design. In a site-generated project the design evolves from a most meticulous analysis of both the visible and invisible aspects of the site. To be considered are its history, its existing features and even the invisible, geological structure beneath it. We were delighted to find a perfect example of site-generated design in a private garden in Devon. It has been created by Jessica Duncan at Kerscott in Swimbridge.

We had always thought that we knew Britain well. After all, we'd been travelling

CONSULT THE GENIUS OF THE PLACE IN ALL

Alexander Pope

around visiting historic gardens and designing new ones for the past eighteen years. During that time we had taken commissions in London and the Home Counties, and design projects had extended to most of the other 'shires' – from Hampshire to Yorkshire and from Kent to Gloucestershire. Incidentally, we have also designed gardens in Ireland, Spain, France and the United States. All this experience served to make us vividly aware that the English gardener is a very special breed, but despite this preparation we were bowled over by the diversity of the gardens we found. Their beauty reflected a high degree of technical expertise – these so-called amateur gardeners were quietly practising horticulture and garden design at a professional level, for no other purpose than their own enjoyment. It became clear that garden and landscape colleges could be made redundant by a good eye and real determination to create a beautiful site.

We soon realised that, despite their diversity, all the gardens on our route had one thing in common. Their owners were all obsessive about gardening. This showed in the immaculate condition of the gardens, often maintained by the garden owner, with no outside help whatsoever. Without armies of gardeners to maintain them and pots of money to support them, these fabulous gardens represented a quintessentially British phenomenon. They are one aspect of an attitude that has spawned so many world-class, revolutionary inventions, later capitalised on by the rest of the world. Let us give a 'Hosanna in the highest' for the divine amateurism of the British! Of course, we must not get too carried away in our praise for the amateur. Two of the greatest contemporary gardens, both in Scotland, were created by professionals: Charles Jencks' Garden of Cosmic Speculation and Ian Hamilton Finlay's Little Sparta.

Finalising the list of gardens to be included in the television series took some doing. When it was done, the BBC asked us to divide the list into categories. The diversity of the sites made this a surprisingly difficult but highly enjoyable task. However, we came up with the broad definitions of 'Traditional', 'Eccentric' and 'Contemporary'. Past experience gave us a good knowledge of each category. Over the past six years we have written two books on contemporary gardens; the first was *Paradise Transformed: The Private Garden for the Twenty-First Century*. This is now being referred to as a classic work on the subject. In 2000, we developed the theme of the contemporary garden further in *Gardens for the Future: Gestures against the Wild*. The research for these two books about gardens at the cutting edge of design made us feel very much at home in the contemporary gardens that we visited. We tend to use the word 'contemporary' rather than 'modern', because we think it is a much more

accurate description. Modern became a historical term in the late twentieth century, not to be confused with the term post-modern, often used to define the style of today.

Strangely enough, some of the most exciting contemporary gardens that we saw had been built within the confines of an archetypal, traditional site. The Tennis Court Garden at Kiftsgate Court in Gloucestershire was one such an example. It is a subtle play on space and form that is made even more exciting by the context of its traditional setting. Waddesdon Manor in Buckinghamshire is another example of a traditional garden that also has elements of cutting-edge design. In this case computer technology has been used to translate complex, contemporary planting schemes into a practical reality. These two sites were thrilling discoveries for the curious gardeners. They proved beyond any doubt that garden design in Great Britain is vigorously alive and incredibly well. It was truly exciting to discover there was no hostile confrontation between traditional and contemporary garden design. Both have 'a song to sing', and the new designs within the traditional gardens of Kiftsgate and Waddesdon are signs of the continuing evolution of garden design in this country.

A few years ago we wrote another book called *Gardens of Obsession*, an experience that proved to be good preparation for visiting

A small shell fountain (opposite) with the cryptic message: 'Caddis Shell, Goddess Shell'; the Classical allusion is obvious.

Moody and misty view of reclaimed cupolas and moat, alas topped up with blanket weed.

There is always something to see in a good garden, whether traditional, eccentric or contemporary. This is a lesson we learnt very early on in our self-training as landscape and garden designers. Obsessive gardeners sometimes fail to see the beauty of their own gardens. They are only aware of the weeds. They have a tendency to mourn the flowers that bloomed two weeks ago, or long for the colours that will fill the borders later in the year. Traditional gardeners often divide their summers into 'the-rose-in-full-bloom' and 'the-rose-out-of-bloom'. It has been our aim to avoid this syndrome, revealing that gardens can be perceived in a completely different way. At Elsing Hall, for example, we arrived just as the roses were going over. The soft, blowsy effect was quite ethereal and probably just as beautiful as the roses at their peak.

Another common psychological trait is to be found among gardeners who have not yet realised their internal vision for the site. They can see the future so vividly, however, that they show visitors around as if the garden were already transformed to reflect their ideal. Is this perhaps a variation on the tale of 'The Emperor's New Clothes'?

Only gardeners who have actually achieved a good proportion of their aims can open to the public. Of course, obsessive gardeners choose their dates carefully, so that their garden will be 'looking its best'. The National Garden Scheme is the main charity

gardens in the 'Eccentric' category of this book. The British have always been good at eccentricity, and these gardens were a fabulous display of that trait in the national character. The eccentric gardens were not confined to England. In Scotland we met a man who described himself as a 'rabid nationalist' and dedicated his time to raising thousands of bedding plants under glass. This year he had chosen the Scottish flag of St Andrew as his design, realised in pretty blue and white violas. In the event of a late spring frost, he would stay up all night, watering his plants to prevent the frost taking hold and destroying his magnificent display.

THE BRITISH HAVE ALWAYS BEEN GOOD AT ECCENTRICITY,
AND THESE GARDENS WERE A FABULOUS DISPLAY OF THAT TRAIT
IN THE NATIONAL CHARACTER.

to benefit from garden opening, and what a splendid organisation it is. Full marks from both of us. The garden owners obviously loved receiving visitors. They lapped up the compliments paid by inquisitive neighbours and others who came to admire, as well as indulging in a little espionage that could help to transform their own gardens.

Whatever category one uses to describe a garden, there is one overriding feature common to all. All gardens are subject to change. Plants, trees and shrubs grow, reach maturity and then die. Every garden is dependent upon its owner. The depth of the owner's passion is usually reflected in the degree of maintenance in the garden. The great landscapes that survive from century to century have architectural elements that can withstand the vagaries of weather, time and even neglect.

We doubt there will be any truly great gardens surviving from the current garden fashion for perennial planting. The use of a multitude of grasses with *Sedum spectabile* and *Rudbeckia fulgida* is a formula which has rapidly become a cliché. It is a boon to low-maintenance gardeners, but we think it is uninteresting and inexpressive as a total design look. On a recent trip to Washington DC, one of the haunts of the grass designer boys, we noticed 'grass as fash' everywhere, from quite good, large-scale plantings around official buildings, to ridiculous, small beds of out-of-scale species creating frills in front of

splendid, late-nineteenth-century stone town houses. Most inappropriate for the architecture and the streetscape. In Britain we found grasses cropping up everywhere, from a stall at a typical village fête in Gloucestershire to the corner of a garden specialising in growing flowers for drying in Scotland. So, the limitless potential for unstructured boredom is spreading to Britain as well.

The summer of 2000 was a wet one in Great Britain and the drop-head hood sometimes had to go up on the drop-dead Alvis that we used for our tour of Britain. Despite the occasional discomfort of a downpour and the considerable distances covered, the making of the programmes was a wonderful experience. Our pilgrimage confirmed the suspicion that the British are the greatest nation of gardeners anywhere in the world, aided and abetted, of course, by the extraordinary temperate climate and fertility of the soil. Just as every garden changes year by year, we hope that the variety of gardens in this book will inspire everyone to look afresh at their own particular patch of Eden. ▼

Gordon Taylor

Guy Cooper

Gardens
Traditional

The two formal canals leading to the double-storey pavilion based on the one at Westbury Court, Gloucestershire.

Every foreigner has a vivid image of the traditional British garden. Their vision is dominated by endless swathes of flowering plants, arranged either in a cottage garden with roses around the door, or in Jekyll-style herbaceous borders. The reality of the traditional garden today is rather different. Sixty years ago a team of twenty gardeners might be employed to maintain the grounds of a large country house. Those days have long gone. Now two gardeners with a ride-on mower may be expected to do the same job. As a result, the herbaceous border has gone hardy perennial and many of the flower-beds have been grassed over.

In the smaller traditional garden change is also rife. The space has to serve as a playground for small children and an exercise area for the family dog. In addition to these difficulties, garden owners have to juggle their time between tending the real garden and watching garden make-over shows on the telly!

These are all very practical considerations, but the traditional garden, whatever its size, still flourishes in Great Britain today. It can be satisfying, beautiful, creative and calming. Very occasionally, perhaps on a couple of days a year, even the owners may feel somewhat satisfied with their own work.

Sugden Water Garden

Water margin plants flourishing on the edge of the pond (above) surrounded by a birch grove.

A series of descending pools (opposite) from the Sugdens' second creation of these water features reflecting their passion for water-loving plants.

Gordon: Let's talk about the weather. Roads bore me.

Guy: That's why you are such a terrible navigator. You don't actually care where we are going, so we don't end up in the right place.

Gordon: It's the arrival, not the journey. No, that's not right ... it's supposed to be the other way round.

The Sugdens bought their house in 1977. The following year they started to garden the field that stretched away from the house. The area was over 180m (200yds) long and in places it was 30m (35yds) wide. There were wonderful views over the North Yorkshire countryside to the White Horse at Kilburn.

They began with the area immediately around the house and rented the field to a local farmer who needed the grazing for some cattle. The Sugdens turned the spoil left by builders into a rockery and two ponds connected by a waterfall and stream. They lined the pools with plastic and imported some Lakeland slate and 20 tonnes (20 tons) of local limestone rocks. Ten years later they rebuilt the whole water system because it had 'never looked natural'.

The Sugdens have learnt a great deal about water in the garden and it now looks completely convincing in the landscape, even though the upper pool is only 5m (6yds) from the house. The stream flows down into a larger pool where Heather satisfies her passion for water lilies. She grows 'Norma Gedye', 'Froebelii' and 'Pygmaea Helvola' with plantings in or near the ponds of sweet and yellow flag, water forget-me-not, flowering rush, *Typha minima*, branched bur-reed, kingcup, golden club, water plantain, cape pondweed, *Villarsia bennettii* and bog bean.

There is enough room in the pond for about seven different types of water lily and these need to be dug up and split every two years. It is a cold and messy job, but Heather says that it is very worthwhile. If they were neglected, the water lilies would grow too big and the entire area of the pond would be covered in their leaves.

As the years went by, the Sugdens progressed further and further into the field beyond the house. Fairly early on they made a sunken garden 90m (100yds) away from the building. They paved it with flagstones bought at fifty pence each from the council and old bricks salvaged from a demolished farmyard. This done, they went on to consider a means of connecting the different spaces. In 1980 they built a pergola approximately 3m (10ft) wide and about 15m (16yds) long. They covered it in wisteria but it was not linked to the rest of the site. They soon solved this problem by planting an irregular course of trees to join the house to the pergola.

The fence that kept the cattle to the furthest end of the field was soon replaced with a golden *Leylandii* hedge. This is now 5m (17ft) tall and has been trained to create a 4.5m (15ft) high archway on an axis with the end of the pergola. This has been achieved by tying the tips of the trees together and carefully trimming them each year.

Eventually the cows were banished and in a naturally boggy area between the *Leylandii* and the edge of the garden, the Sugdens created a bog garden. Here they have planted candelabra primulas, giant cowslips, flowering rush, cotton grass, ostrich fern, monkey musk, *Rheum palmatum rubrum*, *Gunnera manicata*, *Ligularia dentata* 'Desdemona', *Ligularia* 'The Rocket' and Siberian irises.

This garden is an excellent example of what two people obsessed with gardening can do over a twenty-year period with a reasonable amount of space and a fairly limited budget. When you enter the garden now, you are immediately aware of the sound of water and the sky reflected in the ponds. The Sugdens had no formal training in design, and yet looking at their garden proves once again that some enthusiasm, some knowledge and masses of energy are all that are needed when you are faced with an empty site. ▼

Eric and Heather Sugden (opposite) in front of their imposing fifteen-foot-high *Leylandii* arch beyond which is the more informal area of the garden.

Deanswood

DEANSWOOD PLANTS, LITTLETHORPE, YORKSHIRE

Jacky Barber (opposite), a true garden obsessive, in her Yorkshire garden. Her giant 'helper', the Willow Woman, is a reminder of the weeding women whose labour was so useful in grand Elizabethan gardens.

Water is always essential and here a shallow stream (below) has been encouraged to meander through a 'border' of water-loving plants.

Mrs Jacky Barber has lived and gardened on 0.8 hectares (2 acres) for eleven years. At first she and her husband had young children and this left little time for gardening. Time passed, the children grew up and, perhaps most significantly, they gave up riding. This freed the pony field next to the house for the more adult purpose of extending the garden.

By opening up a ditch the Barbers created a small, free-flowing stream. This is now spanned by a bridge which leads from the area near the house to a larger space that is crammed with interesting features. There are herbaceous borders, shrubs, a stream-side garden and three ponds. Moisture-loving plants, such as primula and iris, rodgersia, rheum, gunnera and caltha, grow close to the edge of the water.

Jacky grows numerous varieties of willow which she uses to give shade, to make sculptures and to create willow arbours. The arbours are only 1.5m (5ft) high and they create an intriguing route from one area of the garden to another. A sculpture entitled *The Willow Woman* welcomes you into the main garden. She was going to be a willow man until Jacky found that the figure needed a stronger base. To provide the necessary support the willow trousers became a wider, steadier crinoline and, *voilà*, a willow sex-change sculpture. During the spring and summer the willow lady is clothed in vigorous new shoots. She greets you with a wave of one hand. On her other arm is a basket, a reminder that all gardens, even willow gardens, need constant maintenance.

Jacky sells a wide selection of plants, ploughing the profits back into the maintenance of the garden. On the day that we filmed there, the garden was open for its tenth year running on behalf of the National Garden Scheme. Almost 700 people came and she raised £2,500 for the benefiting charities. Jacky obsession with the garden and shows how that obsession can give layers of enjoyment and pleasure to a public far wider than her personal friends. ▾

Willows are unbelievably fast-growing and flexible. They can be bent to almost any design you might wish as in the willow arbour here.

Endsleigh House

MILTON ABBOT, DEVON

A vigorous watercourse (above) designed by Humphry Repton flows from its reservoir into the Dairy Dell Pond.

Beyond the twenty-seven-room *cottage ornée* (opposite) are the long terraces linking the cottage to the woods designed in the early nineteenth century by Repton.

Gordon: The Duke and Duchess of Bedford hired Repton and Wyatville to design the grounds and this *cottage orné*, which is nothing more than an ornamental cottage.
Guy: Only an ornamental cottage! Many people would say that twenty-seven rooms was quite a lot for an ornamental cottage but if you, as a foreigner, wish to describe it that way – you may!

The Russell family, whose titular head is the Duke of Bedford, have owned a great deal of England for a great many years. Until 1953 they owned an estate of approximately 1,200 hectares (3,000 acres) on the Tamar, the river that divides Devon from Cornwall. In the early nineteenth century the Russells commissioned Humphry Repton to design their estate at Woburn. In 1811 he made one of his extraordinary Red Books for the Endsleigh estate. The book still exists, although it is kept at Woburn, and it shows views of the house before and after his improvements. Repton was only at Endsleigh for five days. A few months later he had an accident in a carriage and never returned to Devon. The Red Book was made during his convalescence.

Repton's sons realised his plans for Endsleigh, incorporating alterations by the architect Wyatville to the *cottage orné*, a substantial mansion which the ducal couple and their many fishing friends needed only during brief periods of residence on the estate.

A long grassy terrace leads from the garden side of the house towards the Shell House and the Grotto. Above this, the Rose and Yew Walks form two further terraces. A long conservatory originally stood on one of the terraces. All that remains is its arcaded retaining wall and some fairly informal planting. The terraces typify the Reptonian aesthetic, for they bring formality to the area immediately around the house. As the nineteenth century progressed, these areas became increasingly complex. Perhaps this was a reaction to fifty years of Capability Brown's informal 'landskip' style.

The Shell House and Grotto were designed by Wyatville and used to display a collection of geological specimens and shells. Beyond them are the extraordinary woods named the Upper and Lower Georgy, after Georgiana, wife of the sixth Duke. It is here that one finds some of the fourteen 'champion' trees which grow on the Endsleigh estate. These are the largest trees of their type in Great Britain, a calculation based on the height and girth of their trunks. In this area they include *Abies normanniana* (Caucasian fir), *Rhododendron* 'Endsleigh Pink', *Fagus sylvatica* 'Pendula' (weeping beech), *Aesculus indica*, (Indian horse chestnut), a specimen of *Kalopanax septemlobus* var. *maximowiczii* and a 35m (115ft) high *Cryptomeria japonica* 'Lobbii' (Japanese cedar).

A LONG GRASSY TERRACE LEADS FROM THE GARDEN SIDE OF
THE HOUSE TOWARDS THE SHELL HOUSE AND THE GROTTO.

On the other side of the house the ground falls away towards the pond in the Dairy Dell and the cottage beside it. Immediately above are the dairy and ice house, both suggested by Repton but designed by Wyatville. The Dell was a very important part of Repton's design. In it he experimented with the use of water. Brought from a source about 1 km (0.5 miles) away, the water is collected in Edgecombe Pond. It then falls into a catch pit, where it is divided into the two channels running down either side of the valley. The water then creates a sequence of small pools, channels, cascades and tiny trickles. The system has recently been restored so that it can all be seen as Repton intended.

Between the Dairy Dell pond and the house there is a rock garden. The picturesque rockery, with its pond and fountain, contains a network of paths notable for their patterned pebble work. One of the paths leads to a rustic underground grotto. Water is again a feature in the rock garden, where it falls over a crag of rock below the grotto to form a cascade.

Repton also designed a Swiss Cottage, another very fashionable feature at the time. It stands on the other side of the Tamar, above the curve in the river. From the Swiss Cottage, which was meant to be no more than a belvedere, there is the most magical view of the entire landscape. A clump of pine trees frames the view, forcing one to look

either to the left or right. To the right is the view of the house, with its wide grass terraces and the amazing woods beyond. To the left the view overlooks the River Tamar, a stretch of silvery water described by Repton in the Red Book as constituting '... the leading feature of the place by an interrupted continuity of glitter'. This dramatic vista shows the true genius of Repton. By gentle engineering, he made nature meet art, creating one of the finest landscapes in Britain today. ▼

The Pond House (above) overlooks the Dairy Dell Pond.

From the Swiss Cottage (opposite) there is a view of the silvery River Tamar 200 feet below, dividing Devon from Cornwall.

Bramham Park

WETHERBY, YORKSHIRE

A gargoyle fountain mask (above), a 'cousin' of those on the grand water staircase in the Boboli Gardens, Florence.

A main axis in Bramham Park landscape (opposite), running up from the Obelisk Ponds to one of the most perfect of eighteenth-century English Gothic summerhouses.

Bramham Park celebrated 300 years of existence in 1998. The house and grounds were originally laid out in the last decade of the seventeenth century and completed in about 1710 by Robert Benson, who became the first Lord Bingley. He was extremely ambitious and was appointed Lord Treasurer to Queen Anne in the same year; she is said to have visited Bramham at least once.

Bingley was also a director of the notorious South Sea Company and after the Bubble burst his carriage was stoned in Cavendish Square, London. Like his neighbour Lord Aislabie, the maker of another great garden at Studley Royal near Ripon, Bingley benefited hugely from the South Sea Company and spent a good deal of his wealth on the creation of the house and gardens at Bramham Park. Nikolaus Pevsner, the famous art historian who made a survey of all Britain's finest buildings between 1950 and 1970, called Bramham 'an Italian villa set in a French château garden'.

Most of Britain's finest seventeenth-century landscapes were swept away in the mid-eighteenth century, at the height of the Picturesque Movement. During this period garden landscapes dating back hundreds of years were erased and the informal became the only acceptable style. These informal, Picturesque landscapes were the context for the eighteenth-century English country house, as designed by the great garden and landscape designer, Lancelot 'Capability' Brown. Bramham is the only truly complete seventeenth-century landscape in Britain to have survived the Picturesque period unscathed.

Lord Bingley took his grand tour in the last decade of the seventeenth century and Bramham is his unique reflection on the villas, châteaux and gardens that he must have seen in Italy and France. He was clearly inspired by the landscape designs of the great André Le Nôtre, the seventeenth-century designer to Louis XIV. At Bramham, Bingley altered the conventional concept of the formal garden by placing the main axis, the grand vista, at ninety degrees to the garden façade of the house. The great gardens of France of the same period were always set at right angles to the palace or château. At Versailles, for example, the main axis runs from the centre of the garden side of the château and is strengthened by a line out to the grand canal which runs on into infinity.

We always think that the formal grandeur of the main axis at Bramham is intrinsically British and rather eccentric. When you stand in front of the house and look to your left you see the most staggering vista. More than a mile long, it draws the eye into the distant landscape and the sky beyond.

At first, the main axes are enclosed by 6m (20ft) tall beech hedges. These widen out to

BRAMHAM PARK IS A GRAND AND UNUSUAL HOUSE, BUT ITS
FORMAL GARDENS ARE GRANDER AND EVEN MORE UNUSUAL.

Professor Nikolaus Pevsner

The Urn of the Four Faces (above) stands at the point where some of the formal beech hedges converge. Carved from Yorkshire stone, it is both a traditional eye-catcher and a means of stopping the view.

Late-seventeenth-century formal landscape grandeur (opposite) depended on the length of the vista, and here it is one mile long with a rotunda and, beyond, an obelisk as focal points.

encompass two square reflecting pools. Beyond the pools there is an *allée* of trees and a classical, pillared rotunda. A 30m (100ft) high obelisk stands at a distance of about 1 km (0.6 miles) from the rotunda, and in certain lights it appears to be resting on top of it. On the lawn below the Gothic Pavilion – designed by Batty Langley in the mid-eighteenth century – are two pools known as the Obelisk Ponds. The Pavilion is still used by the family for summer suppers and picnics. Since it is about 0.4 km (0.25 miles) from the house, a golf cart proves handy for transporting food and drink.

Long *allées* of clipped beech lead the eye

towards other focal points in the garden, such as temples, follies or statues. At one point they converge, creating a site for *The Urn of the Four Faces*. Each face of this amazing piece represents one of the four seasons. Other *allées* lead on from the urn to the T-Pond, or to classical structures in what becomes a 'borrowed landscape'.

There are more than 3.2 km (2 miles) of beech hedges at Bramham. It takes three men five weeks each year to clip them. It is delightful to walk the circuit designed to encompass all of the different formal elements in the park, and it is only by exploring in this way that one starts to get a feel for the landscape's true scale. The park covers almost 28 hectares (70 acres), and is set in a 2,400-hectare (6,000-acre) estate.

Bramham still belongs to the Lane Fox family who built it 300 years ago. It is now their main residence, but the survival of the seventeenth-century park is probably due to the fact that it was originally used only during the hunting season. For many generations the family have looked after the park with great sensitivity and affection. A fire in 1829 rendered the house almost unusable and it remained empty until it was rebuilt by Detmar Blow in 1910. Even during this period of dereliction, the park was beautifully maintained. In 1911 Blow attempted to reconstruct some of Bramham's early-eighteenth-century gardens. ▼

The Orchards

The change of levels (right) is marked by water jets and water cascades.

Jeremy Simpson: I remember constantly talking to my bank manager. When I told him about the garden he said, 'Well, as Guy's a friend of yours perhaps £500 would cover it.'

Gordon: Extraordinary, I thought we did this job *after* the Second World War …

Penny Simpson: And he was being very generous at £500.

Guy: He was; he thought it was at least £400 more than we really needed!

Jeremy Simpson and Guy Cooper have known each other for almost fifty years, having grown up as neighbours in Bristol. A few years ago Cooper went to spend the weekend with Jeremy and his wife Penny in the country cottage that they bought more than twenty-five years ago. The cottage had expanded over the years to match the size of their family. It is now about four times its original size, although the extensions have been cleverly made to look like an accretion of architectural styles built up over the centuries.

Waking very early one morning, Cooper decided to wander through the garden to the summerhouse. It would be an exaggeration to say that he got lost, but the route along meandering paths was a very complex one. As a trainee landscape designer, Cooper had been taught that gardens were 'all about access and exits'. The Simpsons' garden seemed to break all the rules and he wished that he could get down to improving its layout. In 1993 the Simpsons had some building work done and saw it as an opportunity to redesign the garden. To our delight, we were invited to help.

There are good views from the house, but the real panorama can only be enjoyed from the top of the hill. We had to find a design that would draw people away from the garden immediately surrounding the house to the higher ground. Penny defined the style of the new garden by declaring at the outset that she didn't want anything 'pretty'. She wanted what she defined as a 'working' space, 'where lots of children could rush around and play football without worrying'.

The existing garden was built on different levels and this gave us the opportunity to play around with water. It created a link between the lower stone terrace, the upper lawn and the hedge. In the upper lawn we designed a large circular pool with raised sides high enough to sit on and a single jet of water. A yew hedge was planted as a backdrop. On the lower terrace water was again a feature. It was enclosed by stone steps which allow access between the levels. The water issues from a mask, flows down from one pool to another and then through a rill to a circular pool close to the main entrance to the house.

The beech hedges that we planted to enclose many areas in the garden work to direct your route. They can either lead you to the gardens close to the house and the summerhouse, or to an avenue of whitebeam (Sorbus aria 'Lutescens'). The avenue is the route to two small lakes where we planted a mix of evergreen and deciduous flowering shrubs, ensuring that the entire landscape beyond could never be taken in at one glance.

We planted many of the wonderful and highly scented viburnums, both the winter-flowering V. bodnantense and the spring-flowering V. carlesii. There is a narrow stream which runs through a very small valley to one side of the main avenue of trees. It is intriguing to walk up the avenue to the four classical pillars in the distance, embellished with six domes of clipped box.

By walking as far as the lakes and turning towards the more open landscape you reach another of our designs in the garden. This is a quincunx or formal grid of young ornamental pear and crab apple trees which embrace five very ancient apple trees. A quincunx is a pattern whereby trees are arranged in a grid. The corner of each square is marked by a tree, and the fifth stands at the centre. The trees at the centre of each square are ancient apples – all that remains of the original orchard. We were able to incorporate them in the new design, but one day they will have to be replaced as they are already about 150 years old and that seems old enough for anybody.

The garden was completed seven years ago, and everything has matured just as we planned. The whole area is beautifully maintained by one full-time gardener, Patrick Claridge, and a part-timer, both devoted to keeping this charming Gloucestershire garden in prime condition. ▼

Old apple trees, as in the centre, are embraced in a grid design, a formal quincunx, by young trees of pear and crab apple.

Rousham Park

STEEPLE ASTON, OXFORDSHIRE

Inside each of the pedimented arches (above) of the elegant Praeneste Portico is a semi-circular wooden seat for wonderful views of the River Cherwell and beyond.

A friendly, sexy stone satyr (opposite) permanently guards a pond of water lilies and shimmering golden orfe.

Sir Robert Dormer bought Rousham Park and built the house in 1635, and his descendants, the Cottrell-Dormers, continue to live there today. In the early eighteenth century Charles Bridgeman worked on the landscape of the park, but in 1740 William Kent, already a well-known architect, interior decorator and furniture designer, was asked to renovate the house and improve the gardens. The 4 hectares (10 acres) of garden that Kent redesigned for the family is one of his most complete masterpieces still in existence.

Kent was a classical scholar. Encouraged by Lord Burlington, he studied in Italy for some years, where he was much influenced by the paintings of Salvator Rosa and Claude Lorrain. He was not a practical landscape designer like Bridgeman, but was dependent on others to turn his sketches into the detailed plans that underpin the installation of any garden design. He was responsible for introducing apparent naturalism into the constructed landscape, with irregular shapes and serpentine lines. This was a liberation from the formalities inspired by the French Versailles style that dominated the seventeenth-century gardens. At Rousham we see exactly what Horace Walpole meant when he wrote of Kent that 'he leapt over the fence and saw that all nature was a garden'. It remains a magnificent achievement and an early example of the Picturesque, that uniquely British landscape style. Comparatively few of Kent's gardens remain. Many of them were swept away by an even more 'natural' Picturesque style whose high priests were Capability Brown and his successor Humphry Repton.

As you wind your way from open spaces to enclosed areas and back to open spaces, sometimes glimpsing the river, sometimes a distant hilltop crowned with a folly, sometimes a path leading to another glade, you know that this is among the most romantic informal gardens anywhere in Great Britain. Et in Arcadia Ego , 'And I am in Arcadia', the romantic landscape of the Classical gods. Rousham is famous, but there never seem to be too many visitors. This is fortunate, because peace and tranquillity are

A serpentine rill (Watery Walk) (above) runs through this important early-Picturesque landscape; it could be a marvellous representation of William Hogarth's Line of Beauty.

In Rousham's old Victorian vegetable garden (opposite), the main path has a pair of fine perennial herbaceous borders.

essential to an understanding of the landscape.

A house the size of Rousham originally needed extensive vegetable gardens. Some of these were slowly transformed in Victorian times to orchards and long herbaceous borders. In spite of a reduced staff of only three gardeners, the borders are well maintained. There is an enormous quantity of box in this area. This has suddenly become a great problem for the Cottrell-Dormers as it has been attacked by the blight. For some years the Royal Horticultural Society at Wisley has known about *Volutella buxii*, a disease that causes fungi on box, turning some of the leaves brown. It is a problem, but not a major one. Within the last few years a new disease has occurred called Cylindrocladium Blight. This is another fungus which appears to spread by water splash, or by leaf-blowing contact, thereby contaminating the soil below other box plants. It is also spread by people and animals brushing past the hedges. It is almost certain that this new virus is affecting a box arch leading from one area of the garden to another. Mrs Cottrell-Dormer is extremely worried because there are several hundred metres of box hedge, to say nothing of the topiary in that area of the garden. She is horrified by the possibility that the box may be dead within a couple of years, thus denuding an area of her garden

of one of its venerable features.

Nobody ever found a remedy for the Dutch elm disease that killed virtually every elm tree in Great Britain during the 1970s. We do not know whether the same thing will happen to box. The devastation that this would cause in gardens such as Rousham, and all the modern gardens made during the topiary revival of the past ten years, is almost unimaginable. Luckily, the blight is only active in one part of the garden and we must not forget that Rousham's most important landscape is a celebration and evocation of Classical Greece and Rome through that unique English contribution to landscape design: the Picturesque.

CHRIS PARSONS, THE DEW SWEEPER, ROUSHAM PARK

Gordon: How do you feel about this wonderful craft of yours being so short term? So evanescent?
Chris: I don't mind at all, because that's part of the quality of it. It's an original that nobody owns and it's lost forever.

A lawn carpeted in dew and a brush are the only things that Chris Parsons needs to make his exquisite and fleeting patterns. He told us that October mornings produce the best conditions, although it was on a June morning that our zealot director woke us at

The curious gardeners (below) are carefully following Chris Parsons as he completes his ovals in a rectangle.

The team stand triumphantly (opposite) in the middle of a dew-swept lawn transformed in one hour.

4:30 a.m. to see him in action. By 9:00 a.m. we were both ready for lunch! Parsons swept for us just after first light, creating a wonderful, oval pattern of a continuous spiral on a vast lawn on the garden side of Rousham Park.

Although Parsons went to art school, the need to earn himself a crust led to a job in a municipal park. It was through raking up leaves and mowing lawns that he came to sweeping dew patterns. We asked him if he

was influenced by some of the Land Artists of the late twentieth century and he told us that he greatly admires Richard Long and Andy Goldsworthy. The exquisite patterns Parsons brushes out of the dew can be rigidly geometric or wonderfully sinuous. He maintains that anyone can sweep an infinite variety of patterns, unique to themselves. 'Once you do it, you realise how simple it is. I couldn't walk in a straight line at one time. Then I took a job with a local council as a groundsman at a local park. That teaches you to mow in a straight line, I can tell you.'

The best designs are those which have been made on a perfectly smooth bowling green. The other ideal medium is a cricket pitch or a golf green. Parsons also described the optimum weather condition for creating his dematerialising masterpieces: 'You need a clear night for the dew to form, followed by a clear morning with full sun and no clouds. You brush away the dew in parts, and you are left with a design from the sheen of millions of water droplets, until the sun gets hot and burns it away.'

The gardens at Rousham House were designed by William Kent from about 1740. The eighteenth-century poet, Alexander Pope, was devoted to Kent's designs. He once wrote that 'all gardening is landscape painting'. We like to think that Mr Pope and Mr Kent would have approved most heartily of the dew-brushing designs of Mr Parsons.

Headland Garden

POLRUAN, CORNWALL

Guy: How did she plant this?
Gordon: I don't know. Perhaps she has mountain goats as gardeners.
Guy: Must do.

We had no idea what we would find when we set off for the Headland Garden, which clings to the cliff some 30m (100ft) above the Fowey Estuary. The house and garden are built on a small promontory. From a gardener's point of view, the site offers great variety. One side of it, known as the North Coll, is relatively sheltered because it looks on to the estuary. The more exposed side faces the open sea and is known as the South Face.

Inevitably, the main problem all over the garden is wind and salt spray. The wind hits the headland and rises upwards, carrying with it the sea spray in rolling spirals. To survive in this very stressed situation, plants have to be incredibly hardy. Over the years, Jean Hill has frequently seen her plants blown out of the soil. The wind gets behind them, and she can do nothing but watch, helplessly, as they spin out to sea. The winds also affect the depth of the soil. Any top soil that she has tried to add over the years has either been washed or blown away.

Peter Ball (right) has helped over the past twenty-five years to construct and maintain this amazing garden.

Rocks found on the headland have become a path and archway (opposite) to another part of this garden.

Despite all of these difficulties Mr and Mrs Hill have created a wonderful garden. When they bought the Headland twenty-five years ago it was entirely covered in brambles. When these were removed they found a fairly intricate series of paths, connecting stone walls and gateways leading precariously from one level of the cliff to another. These have now been restored and form part of the slightly terrifying but exciting expedition around this true headland garden.

Over the years the Hills have found quite a lot of plants that will grow in these difficult conditions. Among them are griselinia, *Sedum acre* (or biting stonecrop), sea buckthorn, escallonia, phlomis, *Fuchsia magellanica* and some of the hebes. On the North Coll they have been more successful in growing trees such as Monterey pine, mountain ash, purple beech, eleagnus and olearia. On the southern side of the garden Jean grows aloes, echeverias, aeonium and sempervivum. Camellias also thrive, sometimes reaching 4.2m (14ft) and blooming magnificently every year.

Beside the house there is a vegetable garden where potatoes, spinach, sweet corn and courgettes are grown, along with gooseberries, raspberries and black and white currants. All this goes to show that, even in a place as apparently inhospitable as the Headland, an enormous range of plant material can be grown, provided the gardener makes maximum adaptation to the site. Jean's gardening philosophy has become clear-cut over the years: 'I arrived at our present planting scheme after trial and error. This garden has characteristics that mean you just cannot force your likes and dislikes upon it, you just have to go with the flow.'

Jean's husband can no longer help her but they have always had a local man, Peter Ball, to assist with building paths, rebuilding stone walls, and carrying on the day-to-day maintenance. He loves the job and says that he cannot think of a more beautiful place to work anywhere in England.

The Hills originally bought the Headland because Mrs Hill wanted to live in a place where she could sail and swim every day. A hundred steps lead down the North Coll to a little cove, always known as the Girls' Cove, and a further thirty steps lead to a little beach. Mrs Hill, now in her seventies, swims every day during the summer. Starting in May when the water is still bitterly cold, her first swim is probably only 10m (10yds) there and back. At the height of the summer she will swim around the promontory and further out into the estuary, probably 200m (218yds) each day, and this continues until November.

Jean Hill is sometimes known to her close friends as the 'mermaid of Fowey'. When she is out at sea, she can look up at the cliff face rising straight out of the water and see the most exposed part of her garden. ▼

I ARRIVED AT OUR PRESENT PLANTING SCHEME AFTER TRIAL AND ERROR.
THIS GARDEN HAS CHARACTERISTICS THAT MEAN
YOU JUST CANNOT FORCE YOUR LIKES AND DISLIKES UPON IT,
YOU JUST HAVE TO GO WITH THE FLOW.

Hunworth Hall

HUNWORTH, NORFOLK

Henry Crawley (right) in front of his recreated seventeenth-century Dutch-style garden with its canal and formally clipped shrubs.

Overview of the major vista (opposite) from the hall to the landscape beyond.

Gordon: Managing a wild meadow, a medieval mead or the Monet field of poppies is a lot more difficult than just scattering some seed.

Henry Crawley: Ideally you need animals, of course, that's how they managed them originally.

Guy: They were called sheep, I think ...

The Crawley family bought Hunworth Hall in the mid-1960s when it was being sold off by the adjacent Stody Estate. The house was built in about 1700, a period in which English architecture and gardens were greatly influenced by Dutch style as a result of William of Orange's ascent to the throne of England. At Hunworth Hall the Dutch influence can be seen in the charming gable ends of the house and may also have shaped the formal garden which is shown on maps made in 1726. This layout had long gone when the Crawley family bought the house.

By then it had been inhabited by tenant farmers for almost 200 years. The site of the old garden was nothing but a rough paddock. A section of curved fence survives. This was originally put in to keep cattle away from the front of the house.

From the front door of the house the view is shaped by a very long beech *allée* leading to a focal point at the far end. Henry associates this feature with Lutyens. 'It goes back to the old idea of not allowing people to see the whole garden from the front door,' he says. 'It encouraged them to go out.' Also on the main vista from the house are two formal beds surrounded by box hedges. Domes at the centre of the beds are cut from variegated box. Beyond that are two large eighteenth-century urns encircled by clipped cones of yew. The circle can be entered at four points, also marked by yew cones. A beech hedge spanning the whole garden has been given a profile that echoes the Dutch gable ends of the house.

An arched trellis at the end of the main vista of the garden encloses a little door. On it is a notice which reads 'Open Me' and inside is a bottle labelled 'Drink Me'. Beyond that is another little door which opens out on a view of the 'borrowed' landscape of fields and hedges. A little *Alice in Wonderland* joke as the climax to the main axis of this Anglo-Dutch garden.

Two formal canals edged with generous

beds of lavender and 'lollipops' of *Ilex* 'Golden King' are set at right angles to the main axis. At the furthest end of the longer canal is a two-storey pavilion inspired by the garden house at Westbury Court in Gloucestershire. The Hunworth pavilion, although not an exact copy, is also built in red brick and has details in white-painted wood. From its first floor, which can be reached only up a stair at the back of the building, the views across the garden are magnificent. Henry describes it as his '... refuge from gardening. Once you are up there, you sort of distance yourself from your labours and try to relax a bit.' At the end of the second canal there is a pretty one-storey orangery.

Two wild-flower meadows near the house provide a fantastic contrast to the formality of the garden. Henry describes these areas as '... bits of garden that we haven't got at'. He explained that the garden had been fairly wild before he began to formalise it. 'These meadow areas are rather like the native forests of Britain,' he told us. 'They are gradually diminishing, but they are being preserved.'

There are one or two other continental influences in the garden. Beyond the iron railings to the right of the house is a terrace, about 3m (10ft) wide and 12m (40ft) long, where the family may play *boules* if they wish. To add to the continental feeling, there are

terracotta pots filled with agave, a familiar sight in southern France, Italy and Spain.

The garden is looked after by the Crawleys with very little outside help. It is a fairly labour-intensive garden. The hedges are cut by Henry once a year. He can do a big hedge in a 'long, painful day', he told us, 'but I try to do the little ones first, because it's usually the *magnum opus* that finishes me off'. He admitted that the prospect of the BBC filming had prompted him to get some help, but on the whole he and his wife seem more than happy to maintain this very good twentieth-century recreation of what some English gardens looked like at the end of the seventeenth century. ▼

A view from the pavilion (above) to the orangery focal point at the end of the canal vista.

Hunworth Hall's Dutch-style gables (opposite) date from about 1700.

Drumlanrig Castle

THORNHILL, DUMFRIESSHIRE, SCOTLAND

The winged heart (above), the family crest, symbolically represents the heart of Robert the Bruce and his connection with the Douglas family.

Giant Douglas fir, *Pseudotsuga menziesii* (opposite), grown from seed brought back from Washington state by David Douglas, the plant hunter.

Guy: This castle was designed to make people realise how rich and powerful the owners were. They also wanted you to feel a little bit intimidated.

Gordon: Well, that may be the case with you citizens from the United Kingdom, but it ain't the case for a citizen of the United States.

Guy: Keep your Republican notions to yourself, thank you very much Mr Taylor.

Drumlanrig has belonged to the Montagu Douglas Scott family for over 600 years. It is built at the end of a *drum*, Scots for a large ridge or rump of hill. The present castle was started in 1679 by the first Duke of Queensberry and even then it was considered a palace. In the early 1700s the second Duke created the main parterres below the massive retaining walls of the castle. The Rose Parterre, the Upper Parterre and the High White Sand Garden are planted annually by the Duchess. Beyond them is the even more fascinating shadow of the Low Sand Garden which can be traced in the mown grass. This early-eighteenth-century layout is a wonderful relic from Drumlanrig's garden history.

The landscape around the castle covers several hundred acres and was changed during the nineteenth century by the fifth Duke with the help of Charles Mackintosh and David Thomson, two of the most important Victorian landscape architects.

Among the trees to have reached giant maturity are Douglas firs (*Pseudotsuga macrocarpus* and *menziesii*), weeping beech and sycamore.

Not only were a great variety of trees planted on the hills beyond the formal garden, but an extensive network of roads and paths was also made, to enable guests to either walk or take a pony carriage into the woods where they could look back at the magnificent castle from various viewpoints.

Six different huts or follies, known as sitooteries in Scots vernacular, were built at various points through the landscape. The Heather Hut, built in the 1840s, has been restored. It is circular with eight wooden pillars supporting the heather roof. There are very small windows and inside the walls and ceiling are entirely covered in decorative patterns made from various types of dried heathers, birch and dried moss. The centre-piece on one wall is a heather representation of the ducal arms, a flying or winged heart. It represents the heart of Robert the Bruce, taken after his death by his friend Douglas on a pilgrimage to the Holy Land. On his journey Douglas was persuaded to fight the Moors in Spain, but died outside Granada, flinging the heart at the infidels as a final inspiration to his followers. The heir to Drumlanrig, Earl of Dalkeith, who walked around the garden with us, completed the sad story:

'I am afraid they all perished, but as a

Drumlanrig Castle was built in the late seventeenth century to show the riches and power of the Dukes of Queensberry.

Deep in the Drumlanrig forest this Heather Hut (above) was used gratefully by nineteenth-century guests at the castle; the decorative patterns are made from birch, dried heather and mosses.

Parterre restored (opposite) by the present duchess with early-eighteenth-century shadow parterre in the background.

result of this sort of brave and bold gesture, the Douglas family took as its motif the flying heart. It's a most beautiful symbol and it can be seen all over Drumlanrig in lead and stone, and here it is in heather and moss.'

Immediately outside the hut are some of the North American Douglas fir trees mentioned above. They were grown from seed planted in 1831 by the brother of David Douglas, the great plant collector, who was clerk of works at the castle. The trees around the Heather Hut are now so large that they block the original views and the hut has become a little refuge in a dark forest. The Earl was well aware of the problem posed by the trees:

'I think it is one of the great challenges of a garden of this sort. You tend not to notice how the views have disappeared, and when you do notice, you may lack the courage to remove the overgrown trees. The trees are valuable in their own right, but they destroy the overall purpose of the garden.'

He went on to explain that 'years of benign neglect' had resulted in the merging of the garden with the surrounding woodland. If they were to restore the site to its Victorian condition, complete with elaborate parterres and displays of bedding plants, the rather charming relationship between the cultivated landscape and the woodland would be lost. 'I suppose our hope,' he said, 'is to go back to the eighteenth century, when the garden

had cascades linking it to the little burn running along the bottom of the site. Perhaps this is where we should look for clues about what to do in the twenty-first century.'

There are already some plans to open up a number of nineteenth-century vistas. There is still a road leading away from the Heather Hut, across an artificial stream to the highest viewpoint. From a height of 225m (750ft), you look across the wooded landscape to the castle about 0.8 km (0.5 miles) away. The trees screen the lower areas of the garden around the castle in such a way that you only see the recently restored parterre. At the top of the slope stands the grand seventeenth-century castle. It was designed to intimidate passers-by and to impress on the world at large that it belonged to someone very rich and powerful. They were indeed lords, nay, dukes of all they surveyed.

For many generations the family has been extremely successful in maintaining its three great estates, two in Scotland and one in England. Over the years an incredible collection of art has accumulated around them. Today the grounds and castle are open to the public and, immaculately maintained and preserved from century to century, they serve as a reminder of the grander days of power and responsibility. ▼

'YEARS OF BENIGN NEGLECT' HAD RESULTED IN
THE MERGING OF THE GARDEN WITH THE
SURROUNDING WOODLAND.

Ferguson Garden Seminar

AYLESBURY, BUCKINGHAMSHIRE

Hardy geraniums (above), those extremely tough and useful plants, were the Sow 'n' Grow topic the day we saw the garden.

A rediscovered path (opposite) leads to a *trompe l'oeil* fountain framed by a trellis arch.

The Fergusons moved from Kent to a town house in Aylesbury in 1994. They bought a house with a garden on heavy clay approximately 18m (60ft) wide and 42m (140ft) long. The previous owners had no interest in gardens and seemed to have cut what might have been the lawn about three times a year. The Fergusons, however, were devoted gardeners and started redesigning the site a year after they arrived. At first they thought that the only two things in the garden worth saving were a beautiful copper beech close to the garden side of the house and a tall lilac swathed in brambles. This was before they had uncovered a lovely curved paved path on the left-hand side of the garden. This became the site of the pergola. Today it appears to have an intriguing water feature at its far end. Closer examination reveals that it is a *trompe l'oeil* mural.

The garden also contains a beautifully maintained vegetable patch, a small greenhouse and a pond close to the house which provides both the sound of water and its reflection. The fence around the perimeter of the garden is covered in ivies which one day may be completely mixed with clematis and honeysuckle. Near the house is a wide, paved terrace where Sandra and Barry Ferguson can sit and relax.

All the members of the seminar have studied horticulture in some form and they find their regular meetings most stimulating.

Only half an hour's gossip is allowed before the proper meeting starts and another half an hour's natter is permitted about two hours later over sandwiches and drinks. The club has been running for two years and we did wonder if they might soon run out of topics for their meetings. The members set our minds at rest on that point. It was generally felt that they could 'do' a subject more than once: 'At our age we will have forgotten anyway,' said one of them brightly.

As bird lovers, the Fergusons try to use as few chemical sprays and slug pellets as possible. They have tried using bran to encourage the slugs, which in turn encourages the birds to come along and eat them. A misunderstanding about the type of bran suited to this purpose led the husband of one of Sandra's friends to go to Sainsbury's and buy enormous bags of Allbran. He scattered it around his hostas and he swears to this day that the slugs steered clear of them!

It seems incredible that the Fergusons have only been in their house for seven years. The garden already feels mature – a sensation strengthened by the magnificent copper beech that they inherited. Recently the garden was open to the public under the National Gardens Scheme. The Fergusons raised almost £1,000 for that extremely important charity. Sandra loves the one day each year when like-minded gardeners come around her garden and congratulate her upon her achievement.

WE SHALL BE GARDENING AT A HUNDRED ...
        KEEPS YOU FIT AND YOUR BODY ALERT ... WE DO QUIZ EACH OTHER
IN THE WINTER TIME AND THAT KEEPS THE MIND GOING ...
        OH GOD, THOSE LATIN NAMES ...
BUT YOU DO SEE LOTS OF OLD GARDENERS, DON'T YOU?

Positive opinions from the Ferguson Garden Seminar

Cottage Herbery

BORASTON, WORCESTERSHIRE

Dividing two counties here (above), the shady stream encourages herbs like comfrey.

The cottage (opposite) overlooks beds of herbs which are close enough to be used regularly in the kitchen.

Guy: Just being in a place where there are lots of herbs, the sound of water, the scent of wild garlic, it's extraordinarily evocative, don't you think?

Gordon: It's called a trip down memory lane, but we don't want to travel down that lane too far, do we Guy?

At the age of fifteen, when her teacher had asked her to write an essay on herbs, Kim Hurst bought herself a pot of parsley. The purchase, made more than twenty-five years ago, changed her life.

We met Kim briefly in the early 1980s, when we were co-directors of the Herb Society and she came to use the Society's library in London. Visiting the cottage that she and her husband found soon afterwards on the Worcestershire-Shropshire borders was a bit of a trip down memory lane for us. Our home twenty-five years ago was the Tumblers Bottom Herb Farm near Bath. It had a pretty stream at the bottom of the garden, very similar to the Corn Brook which divides Worcestershire from Shropshire and also serves as a division between the growing and display areas of this garden. The sound of water and the scent of wild plants and herbs on the breeze were wonderfully evocative.

It took fifteen years for Kim and Rob to transform the wilderness into this fascinating selection of herbs. Along a main path herbs are grown informally, to emphasise their shape, height, colour and leaf texture. The path leads from the high ground on which the cottage stands, down to the stream and across the bridge to the kind of open, level, south-facing plot that is ideal for most herbs. Here, Kim has made a formal area of raised beds with wooden edges approximately 15cm (6in) high. The beds are about 0.9m (3ft) wide and 1.8m (6ft) long and provide a very good system for growing and gathering herbs. This raised-bed method is particularly suitable in a small garden where herbs with invasive root systems, such as mint and comfrey, must be contained.

Near the raised beds is an intriguing circle marked with stone carvings of the signs of the zodiac. Some of the herbs associated with the planetary signs are also connected to the sixteenth-century 'Doctrine of Signatures' codified by an Italian called Giambattista della Porta. It was believed that the appearance of a plant defined its medicinal properties. The liver-shaped leaves of the hepaticas (liverwort), for example, were deemed good for curing diseases of the liver; similarly, pulmonaria (lungwort) with its spotted leaves was thought to eradicate disease spots on the lungs.

The Cottage Herbery catalogue lists approximately 500 plants, described as 'hardy perennials, herbs, native plants and aromatic plants of quality'. When we were

directors of the Herb Society, we were often asked for our definition of a herb. Kim has no trouble answering this question. In her book a herb is 'a plant that will give me flavour, give me fragrance and give me pleasure'. Most herbs need very well-drained soil. There are also some shade-loving plants and others thriving on the moist banks of the stream, such as comfrey, an important medicinal herb, and meadowsweet.

The display garden was planned mainly for Kim and Rob's own enjoyment, but visitors are encouraged to come on Sundays during May and June. They can learn a great deal about herbs as they wander along the enchanting paths linking one area with another. We hope that the Hursts make a point of reminding them of the cardinal rule when planting a herb garden: if the herbs are within 4.5m (5yds) of the kitchen, you will cook with them every day. Within 9m (10yds), you will use them once a week. Any further, and you can say proudly that you have a herb garden, but the last thing you will do is use it! ▼

People usually think of herbs as low-growing plants, like the boxwood and lavender in the foreground (opposite), but some can grow to six feet high.

Newland Cricket Club

NEWLAND, WORCESTERSHIRE

Some vehicles never die and this roller (above) has been used for almost fifty years.

This cricket pitch (opposite) for two batsmen needs three people to care for the grass.

A brief history of that most English of sporting activities from Hutchinson's Encyclopaedia:

'Cricket is England's national summer game, played with a bat and ball. Its origin is obscure, but some form of bat and ball game has been played since the thirteenth century. In 1711 Kent played All-England, and in 1735 a match was played between teams chosen by the Prince of Wales and the Earl of Middlesex.

'The Marylebone Cricket Club (MCC) was established in Thomas Lord's ground in Dorset Square in 1787, and in 1814 moved to St John's Wood. Since then it has been the controlling authority and its ground the acknowledged headquarters of the game. The first rules of the game were drawn up in 1774. Only underhand bowling was allowed at first, but overarm bowling was introduced in 1865. A batsman stands at each wicket and the object of the game is to score more runs than the opponents. Games comprise either one or two innings per team. Every year a series of Test Matches are played among member countries of the Commonwealth, where the game has its greatest popularity: Australia, India, New Zealand, Pakistan, the UK, Sri Lanka and the West Indies. Famous grounds, besides Lord's, include Kennington Oval and Old Trafford (Manchester).'

The Newland Cricket Club was founded at a meeting in Newland's Swan Inn on Sunday, 5 May 1957. One of the founding members was Richard Hinds who took on the responsibility of groundsman, assisted by Chris Genever, as well as becoming a member of the club. He told us that after the initial mowing, their cricket pitch needs the following attention and programme of care:

'Then you rake the grass up to get all the little tufts. Then I cut it. After that, you do exactly the same thing again, about three or four times in a week. You have to. Then finally, on the Thursday before the match, you use the shaver, and that takes the grass down to a very, very small amount so there is hardly any grass left on the wicket at all. So all my hard work of growing the grass goes in one week. I've never quite understood the theory of it myself. But it works. The season finishes in September. Then I get four months' rest.

'But it's a wonderful scene. On a summer's day, people will go down to the bottom near the stream with their cameras for we've got the wonderful Malvern Hills in the background, absolutely wonderful. I really enjoy it. It's the reason why I continue playing. I love to come out here, it's quiet, it's peaceful and I can get on and do something without any interruptions of the modern world. I love it. Nothing like cricket.' ◆

BASICALLY THE WHOLE THING IS THAT I HAVE TO

CUT THE CRICKET GROUND WITH THAT MOWER THERE, FIRST OF ALL.

Richard Hinds, groundsman

Ecob Garden

ASTLEY CROSS, WORCESTERSHIRE

Nothing is wasted in this garden: from the plants inherited from Michael Ecob's grandparents to yesterday's *Daily Telegraph*.

Only Ecob's favourite newspaper (opposite) disintegrates slowly enough to nurture his vegetable patch.

Gordon: Let me try the swoe ... Yes, this is called inter-active, this is called participation. Look, I am swoeing. Look mother, I'm swoeing!

Michael Ecob: Dare I tell him that those plants are worth 75 pence each?

Guy: No. And we've already lost £1.50.

Michael Ecob found his house through a chance remark made at the best butcher's shop in Stourport. He lives in a medium-sized house in Astley Cross with a garden large enough to fulfil his highest expectations of gardening.

Ecob was born in Rutland and came from a long line of enthusiastic gardeners. Many of the plants in his garden came from relations. The whitebells were from his great-grandmother's house between Burleigh and Cottesmore in Rutland, where there is an RAF station today. He has taken the whitebells with him every time he has moved house. 'The great joy now,' he says, 'is when the Harriers or Tornadoes are flying low. I always think they are coming to take the whitebells back!' Sam, who was a friend of his father's and head gardener at the Billington Estate in Shropshire, gave Ecob some fabulous Michaelmas daisies. The local vet's wife supplied him with the seeds of the giant biennial echium, which was already up to 2m (6ft 9in) when we visited in May.

The house is part of a post-Second World War bungalow estate development. From the front there is no indication of the size of the garden, although the house is larger than its neighbours. The garden is screened on one side by a long line of *Cupressus leylandii*, that extremely controversial hedging plant.

There are no strong divisions between the ornamental plants in the garden and the vegetable patch. Ecob has an inventive mind. The vegetable rows are spaced so that they exactly accommodate the pages of the *Daily Telegraph* that he uses as a mulch. Presumably, a tabloid would be just too insubstantial to do the job. The sheets of newspaper suppress the weeds and as it disintegrates it acts as an

An amazing display of perennial plants (opposite) representing three generations of English cottage gardening.

ideal soil conditioner as well. Over the years Ecob has noticed that the people with the best vegetable gardens always keep poultry or pigeons. 'You know,' he says, 'that's a tip for anybody, have pigeons. Their dung is a wonderful form of organic nitrogen.' All this knowledge must help when it comes to growing the giant vegetables that Ecob enters for local competitions.

In his armoury of garden tools, Ecob has a swoe, a sideways hoe. He first saw one in 1950, while he was still at college. 'I thought it was a horrible thing,' he says. 'I believed that nobody would ever use one.' Thirty years later, he has found that he can't live without his swoe. It allows for very close weeding, among young plants in particular, and the soil can be simultaneously loosened, in elegant, controlled, sweeping side-to-side movements. Ecob finds his swoe the most useful implement in the garden and he deplores the fact that they are now so difficult to buy.

Ecob is master of all he surveys. Perhaps it was his acquaintanceship with Percy Thrower, Britain's first television gardener, that led him to become the local gardening guru. A new lady friend reported that she was gratified to have risen sufficiently in his esteem to be allowed to do some watering in the early morning and late evening. She hoped that she might soon be allowed to mow the lawn! ▼

Hampton Court

HOPE-UNDER-DINMORE, HEREFORDSHIRE

A thatched variation on a traditional hermitage (above) perches perilously above colossal glacial-inspired boulders which arrived 'yesterday'.

View from the tower (opposite) of this new and expensive garden of homage to the Arts and Crafts style.

Guy: Look down there, there's a great *allée* made through the wheat by a tractor. It could be an eighteenth-century landscape.

Gordon: That's not really an *allée*, it's a track through the wheat. I thought it had been decided that an *allée* is a double row of trees.

Guy: Doesn't have to be. An *allée* is something which leads your eye along and through.

Gordon: Just because there are two wheel tracks, it don't make an *allée*.

Hampton Court in Herefordshire is a red sandstone castle with a long and eventful history. At one point it was owned by the Arkwrights, the cotton mill magnate family. The most recent chapter in its story began in 1994 when Robert and Judy van Kampen, an American tycoon and his wife, bought the 400-hectare (1,000-acre) estate. They decided to restore the castle and improve the 8 hectares (20 acres) of parkland and 3.2 hectares (8 acres) of garden.

At the end of the eighteenth century Humphry Repton is said to have designed the Picturesque landscape on the garden side of the castle. The park, which runs down to the River Lugg, is being restored to its late-eighteenth-century condition. Sometimes it seems as though all late-eighteenth-century landowners, inspired by their experiences on the Grand Tour, wanted to create their own version of the Roman *campagna* with inbuilt allusions to the paintings of Rosa, Lorrain and Poussin. What is now seen as the English landscape was actually entirely man-made in a style devised to invoke memories of a foreign land.

'Make it beautiful' was the real message of the van Kampens' gentle brief to Simon Dorrell, the brilliant young painter, draughtsman and garden designer that they commissioned to renew the park and garden. With the help of estate manager Ed Waghorn and his large team, he has created some of

'MAKE IT BEAUTIFUL' WAS THE REAL MESSAGE OF
THE VAN KAMPENS' GENTLE BRIEF TO SIMON DORRELL,
THE BRILLIANT YOUNG PAINTER, DRAUGHTSMAN AND
GARDEN DESIGNER.

Yet another late-nineteenth-century Gertrude Jekyll border (opposite) installed at the end of the twentieth century!

the most extraordinarily complex historically inspired gardens to be built in Great Britain for many years. The van Kampens are devout fundamentalist Christians, and no doubt earnest young students from the USA will come here to improve their souls.

Over the last six years the two very large walled gardens have been transformed. Both were originally put down to vegetable production. In one of them vegetables will still be grown to feed the students who will live in the house while attending courses and conferences. In the second walled garden the main incidents pay homage to nineteenth-century Arts and Crafts design. In the centre there are two large, octagonal pavilions of beautifully crafted English oak. They are set on a canal with a series of waterfalls designed to inspire relaxation and meditation.

The design of the garden echoes a range of different periods. An avenue of limes evokes the seventeenth century, rose and herb parterres are reminiscent of sixteenth-century knot gardens, and a fine herbaceous border is plainly inspired by the very best twentieth-century designs of Gertrude Jekyll. What a pity that there is nothing intrinsically twenty-first century to be found anywhere on the site.

Just beyond the second walled garden is a four-storey tower built in stone and surrounded by a maze. From the top of the tower there is a fine view over the yew maze, which incorporates various Christian symbols and the owners' initials in its design. The view is reminiscent of an eighteenth-century Kip and Knyff engraving, the inspiration of so much of the gardens. Stone steps lead from the ground floor of the tower and into a dark tunnel. The tunnel is curved so that you cannot see the exit. This journey into the dark symbolises the journey of faith. A faith which is rewarded as you round the corner and see sunlight at the far end of the tunnel. The tunnel ends in the Sunken Garden, with its pool and lavish planting of ferns. The enormous boulders that surround the pool appear to have been deposited during the Ice Age, but actually arrived last year.

The energy and artistic skill of the designer combined with substantial funds has enabled a fantasy to be turned into reality in these extraordinary gardens on the Welsh Borders. Mr van Kampen died recently, but his family intend to continue the amazing reconstruction of the landscape around Hampton Court. ▼

His and Hers Garden

A *cordon floriale* of thorny climbing roses (below) on a sturdy trellis divides the His and Her Gardens.

His Garden (opposite) is a large regiment of stakes never entirely camouflaged by the cash crop of dahlias.

Gordon: May I ask how long you have been married?

Sue Wright: We have been married thirty-five years.

Gordon: I would say that's successful. Is it because you have a large garden that you have a long marriage?

Sue Wright: I think it speaks volumes, yes.

The Wrights live in a very attractive Queen Anne house in the appropriately named Quainton village. The house was bought by Mr Wright's mother in 1963, although a large corner of the garden was retained by the Church Commissioners as the site of the new rectory. Mrs Wright only used the house at the weekend and had comparatively conventional ideas about its design and upkeep. Her gardener, on the other hand, was less conventional. When she came home unannounced on a Monday afternoon she found him in her bath with his girlfriend! All this changed when Beric and Sue came to live in the house in 1983. This was the beginning of a loving and, at times, not so loving conflict in the garden. The problem was solved when they accepted the need to develop a 'His and Hers' Garden. Luckily, the garden was large enough to give both of them a decent plot and, as Sue herself says, they now find that they 'can tolerate each other's passions'.

A long trellis fence of roses divides the garden in two. This means that the Wrights do not have to see each other's patches! In Her Garden there is a long herbaceous border and other areas are given over to roses or perennials. It is a space in which Sue can indulge her great passion for different flowers, their species, colours and scents. She combines them to ensure that her part of the garden is beautiful for many months of the year. Some of her favourite flowers are hellebores, lungworts, primulas, honesty, *Crambe cordifolia* and the Russell hybrid lupins. The trellis dividing Her Garden from His is covered in climbing roses.

Beric sees productivity as the sole motive for gardening. It follows that a large area of His Garden should be given over to

vegetables and other useful plants, such as dahlias which can be sold from the stand by the front door. He plants between one and two hundred dahlias each year. The position of each tuber is marked with a 1.2m (4ft) stake so that the emerging plants can be tied up easily and thus produce better flowers for sale. Asked to explain his devotion to dahlias, Beric says: 'They are garish, they are many coloured, they are good natured and they last for a long time.' Sue hates the stakes, hates the colours and loathes dahlias. Although she has persuaded him to change the varieties of dahlia every three years, she still has to put up with some tubers 'mouldering away in the cellar winter after winter'.

The vegetables Beric grows are all the ones you might expect: potatoes, cabbages, spinach, beans, peas and some tomatoes. The crop exceeds anything that a couple who have been married for thirty-five years could possibly expect to eat. Some are sold, some given to the children and others to neighbours. Others, of course, just rot. None of this matters, because growing and looking after them fulfils Beric's vision of the purpose of gardening.

Late in the afternoon, we all gathered together in the kitchen for a comparatively amicable drink. He and She confess that despite conflicting interests in the garden, they are delighted with the solution that they have found. ▼

Her Garden (opposite) is a triumph for many months of the growing year of aesthetic pleasure from perennials.

Romantic Garden Nursery

SWANNINGTON, NORFOLK

Guy: What an entrance, what scale that topiary would give.

Gordon: Yes, even to a one-storey, small ex-pigsty in the middle of the country somewhere.

Guy: A pigsty, Gordon?

Gordon: Well, you know what I mean ... a dream-house-to-be.

A most romantic event involving topiary took place at the Palace of Versailles on 25 February 1745. A masked ball was held in the Hall of Mirrors, and Louis XV and six of his courtiers marched into the party completely disguised as yew topiary – they must have looked a bit like stylised chess men. It was on this occasion that the King wooed Madame de Pompadour, who became his lover and the official court mistress. Perhaps she was overwhelmed by his topiary transformation, for she was also a highly accomplished gardener.

Topiary has undergone a huge revival in the late twentieth and early twenty-first century. It is now so popular that it is used both in the formal garden, its natural design habitat, and in the informal garden, where it creates a pleasing contrast. When we visited

Matched pairs of topiary bay (right), box and ivy welcome the customers.

Examples of the ancient art of topiary (opposite): both animals and geometric shapes.

the Romantic Garden Nursery and talked topiary with John Powles, he agreed that the desire for instant gardens had done much to make topiary popular. Topiary can be bought ready-made in pots and combined to create an instant effect. The nursery is slowly building up its own stock, but Powles continues to buy in plants of all ages and sizes from the continent.

Topiary is not cheap, and nor should it be. By the time it is ready to be sold, it will already have been watered, fertilised and pruned for a couple of decades. Apparently, Powles' customers often neglect the plants after they buy them. They then complain that growth has not been as fast as predicted. All things considered, a clipped bay tree at 3m (10ft) high and some thirty years of age sold at £900 is not expensive. It is, after all, a splendid and unique specimen.

As we watched, Powles, with secateurs in hand, created a topiary spiral from a vaguely shaggy, cone-shaped box. 'You can't go to any plant and cut any shape,' he told us. 'You've either got to have a shape in mind and then select a plant that will create it, or you've got to take your shape from the existing plant'. The process is similar to that of a sculptor visualising the potential in a block of stone. The shapes that he comes up with can be anything from animals, such as foxes, bears and peacocks, to the basic geometric shapes of a formal garden: spirals,

cones, balls, standards and cubes. Having clipped a spiral from box, he outlined the care programme for it over the next few years:

'We'd probably clip it again in about a month's time, having let the light into it. It will become green and it will shoot out, the next two to three years, really thicken it up, then grow the top a bit taller and develop it all a bit further with a healthy diet of water and fertiliser, and then it's finished and waiting for the lucky customer.'

The nursery also supplies topiary cut from azalea, berberis, cotoneaster, syringa, osmanthus, viburnum, *Prunus lusitanica* or Portuguese laurel and some of the small-leaved ligustrum, or privet. ▼

Davies Garden

MADRESFIELD, WORCESTERSHIRE

Some tidy gardeners like Diane Davies (above) like very very tidy plants such as these bonsai.

One of the pleasures of English village gardens (opposite) is that they often have wonderful views of the countryside beyond.

Gordon: There's a question Guy and I have been burning to ask. The glasshouse is so tidy, which is tidier, the glasshouse or the inside of your house?

Diane Davies: Generally, the inside of the house is probably tidier than the glasshouse.

Gordon: Oh! That makes us feel so much worse!

Diane Davies and her husband Peter have lived in the village of Madresfield for more than twenty-five years. Peter is part of the staff at Madresfield Court, with special responsibility for building maintenance. When they arrived they had four children and a succession of puppies. The garden was largely laid down to vegetables, with a small patch of lawn. The children grew up, as did the puppies, and Diane started to spend much more time in the garden. Over the past twelve years it has been completely transformed.

The garden is on the west side of the house and is about 4.5m (15ft) wide and 24m (80ft) long. A low, open fence on the far side of the site allows a wonderful vista over the fields and trees of the park of Madresfield Court – Diane's 'borrowed' landscape.

Diane's father was a very keen gardener and some of the flowers, such as the phlox, originally came from his garden. The hibiscus, camellias and oleanders also came from family or friends. The garden has

grown gradually over the years. Two new rockeries were added, and then a fish pool. The pool was a challenge on this sloping site. Small boulders of Malvern stone had to be set at the back to compensate for the slope. The pool is often visited by a local heron on his fishing expeditions. The pergola above the pool was added in 1996. The sound of the water flowing down the boulders and into the pool is most soothing

All this work was not enough for Diane. In the greenhouse she has a fine collection of auriculas, started when a man who came to paint the house lent her a book on the subject, and she fell instantly in love with these exquisite plants. Now, as a member of the Auricula Society, she is constantly adding to her collection, seduced again and again by the enchanting range of the rich greyed colours reminiscent of an Italian fresco.

Another of Diane's obsessions is her collection of bonsai, started twelve years ago when her son acquired a single tree. He has left home, but the collection now runs to twenty or thirty specimens, which she constantly shapes and restrains. This is the garden of a woman who loves order. She finds that her need for control can be much better satisfied in the garden than the house. The house may be neat and tidy, but the garden is where her heart resides. ▼

Fairhaven

FAIRHAVEN WOODLAND & WATER GARDENS, SOUTH WALSHAM, NORFOLK

George Debbage, the waterman (above), is clearing a dike (Norfolk waterway) with a local rake, a crome, used by his family for three generations.

Britain's largest collection of naturalised candelabra primulas (opposite) grow here and are reflected in the gently moving waters.

Guy: Look at this dappled path.
Gordon: It's like walking through a watercolour, although it is a bit bright.
Guy: Too bright for watercolour? It must be an oil.
Gordon: Yes, I think it is – not that *you* look like an oil painting, of course.

Most people associate Norfolk with the Broads, areas of water created in the Middle Ages when vast amounts of peat were dug out from the indigenous wetlands. The lakes are part of the system of the meandering rivers, the Yare and the Bure. Anyone may sail on the Broads leading to the Fairhaven Estate but you can't land.

The 72 hectares (180 acres) of garden and woodland attached to the house in which the second Lord Fairhaven lived were created by him over a period of thirty years. He was responsible for clearing the tangled wilderness between the hall and the broad and directing and redirecting a network of narrow waterways and drainage channels, known as dikes, and planting the flowers that grow along the paths today, including the largest collection of naturalised candelabra primulas in the country. He was helped by George Debbage, who is now employed by the Fairhaven Trust to look after the landscape. Debbage is a third-generation Norfolk waterman. He never intended to become a gardener. When a job came up on the estate in the winter of 1963, he told himself that he'd stick at it until the snow melted. That was thirty-seven years ago.

In the early spring all the channels or dikes have to be cleared of the debris that has been left over from the year before. This is done by using a large, hooked rake called a crome. Sometimes the residue has to be burnt but often the collection of leaves and other plant material is used as instant compost along the edges of the dikes. John Crome was a famous painter, a contemporary of Turner, who came from Norfolk.

Along these waterways and under the trees 30,000 candelabra primulas (*Primula japonica*), the common spotted orchid and ligularia have taken root. The water margins are marked by the egg-yellow splashes of *Lysichiton americanus*, the dramatically sexy and smelly American skunk cabbage. Another very dramatic plant naturalised here is the extraordinary giant lily, *Cardiocrinum giganteum*, which grows to 3m (10ft), and has horizontal white trumpets springing from the top of its stems. The trees have been planted in such a way that they give shade but allow the sun to shine through and dapple the paths between the lawns around the house, the small rivulets and the wide broads. ▼

Swan mussels unique to the
Norfolk Broads are returned to
the waters where they can be
food for the otters.

Gardens
Eccentric

A fifteen-foot-high sculpture (opposite) made of metal wheels from a farm in which nothing was ever chucked out.

The Penguin Dictionary of Psychology defines obsession as 'Any idea that haunts, hovers and constantly invades one's consciousness. Obsessions are seemingly beyond one's will and the awareness of their inappropriateness is of little or no avail.' In our research for the eccentric gardens in the book we came up against a grand and colourful variety of private obsessions among garden owners.

Eccentric gardens are almost always associated with an owner's overwhelming passion, either for a particular plant species or for a specific vision of landscape. We met one gardener who had no garden in the accepted sense. He had a plastic tunnel full of half-hardy insect-eating plants from the swamps of the Carolinas in the USA. Another grew only cacti and succulent plants, usually found in semi-tropical climates. Among them are agaves with needle-like ends to the growing tips of the thick, tough fleshy leaves, hardly user-friendly.

The truly eccentric gardener is not immediately obvious. It is only when you are allowed into the 'sacred grove' and the conversation begins that you realise how effortlessly all the usual gardening skills can be translated into tools for the creation of a parallel universe.

Bolton Percy Churchyard

BOLTON PERCY, YORKSHIRE

As the perennials are allowed to grow untrammelled (right) they make the churchyard a haunting place in whatever light.

With the church in the background (opposite) and the cemetery seen through the dappled sunlight, this could be a scene from an inspiring Pre-Raphaelite painting.

The cemetery in the enchanting Yorkshire village of Bolton Percy covers 0.3 hectares (0.75 acres) and stands on the opposite side of the road from its splendid parish church. Over several years Roger Brook, a lecturer in horticulture at Askham Brian College near York, has acted as saviour to the cemetery. When he discovered it in 1980 the graves were hidden by a wilderness of weeds. The nettles had grown so high that even the upright crosses were concealed. The recumbent gravestones had vanished under thickets of ground elder, horsetail and bindweed.

Organic gardeners should avert their eyes from this stage of the story, for in the early years Brook made abundant use of herbicide to control the weeds. 'They were so well established,' he told us, 'that I probably sprayed four times during the first year.' After only two years of this treatment the most troublesome weeds had been eradicated and wild flowers and bulbs had started to grow through the mat of dead foliage. There

were daffodils, hyacinths and snowdrops that had been choked off by the coarse vegetation. Wild flowers like celandines and herb Robert also began to flourish. Under the dead weeds he found rich soil, so he scattered seeds of his favourite perennials and planted roses and other rooted cuttings from his own garden.

Brook's method has been to control unwanted species in the spring and autumn, by hoeing, judicious use of herbicides, hand weeding and skimming with a spade. In this way he encourages all the desirable plants to grow profusely. The system seems to work perfectly. When we visited in early summer we found an informal tumble of foxgloves, *Alchemilla mollis*, bright perennial geums, geraniums and tall verbascums. Brook says that the cemetery only needs 2.5 hours maintenance each week, every week of the year.

Brook's controlled commotion of foliage and colour has transformed the site into the most unusual and attractive cemetery we have ever seen. It is a joyful place. The dense undergrowth of flowering hardy perennials is almost as tall as the crosses above the gravestones. Locating your ancestors must be quite a task in high summer. The entire site is still used as a cemetery but there is a small open lawn at the far end where new graves have been made. The lawn adjoins a quiet meadow where sheep were showing that they may safely graze .

WHEN HE DISCOVERED IT IN 1980
THE GRAVES WERE HIDDEN BY A WILDERNESS OF WEEDS.

Wakefield Prison

WAKEFIELD, YORKSHIRE

Lynda Bedford, assistant to the Governor of this high-security prison (opposite) in front of the famous mulberry tree which has been there for about 400 years.

Wakefield Prison was founded as a house of correction through the foresight and generosity of one man, George Savile, who died in London in December 1594. He also left money for the Queen Elizabeth Grammar School.

Wakefield Prison is today one of the three high-security prisons in Great Britain and has almost 800 inmates, the majority serving life sentences. It stands in the centre of the town and it is a very dull, grim place. Inside the high prison walls and the razor wire most of the buildings are late Victorian, five storeys high and as grim, Dickensian and unwelcoming as one would expect a prison to be. There is a grid network of wires approximately 4.5m (15ft) high covering all of the open spaces in order to stop any unexpected helicopters dropping by to pick up the inmates.

At the far end of the prison yards, close to one of the outer walls, is a mulberry tree. It is said to have been there since the prison was founded at the end of the sixteenth century. Mulberry trees were being imported at that time because James I was keen to encourage the silk industry in England. The tree has undoubtedly been there for an extraordinarily long time. Its trunk is extremely large and ancient. It is clear that on occasion branches have broken off and new branches have grown. It is quite likely that this is the very mulberry tree around which the nineteenth-century women inmates danced (forced exercise) in the winter singing the song that almost every child still knows:
'Here we go round the mulberry bush, the mulberry bush, the mulberry bush,
Here we go round the mulberry bush on a cold and frosty morning.'

ALSO I GIVE TWENTIE POUNDES FOR AND TOWARDES
THE BUILDINGE OF A HOUSE OF CORRECTION WITHIN
SEAVEN MILES OF WAKEFIELD FOR THE SETTING OF
THE POORE ON WORKE OR TOWARDES A STOCKE FOR THE
KEEPING OF THEM IN WORKE ACCORDINGE TO THE STATUTE
IF SO BE THERE ANY SUCH HOUSE BUILDED WITHIN THE
SPACE OF TWO YERES NEXT AFTER MY DECEASE AND IF
THERE BE NOT THEN THIS BEQUEST UTTERLIE TO BE VOID.

George Savile, bequest for Wakefield Prison, 1594

Paul and Jackie Gardner Plants

MADLEY, HEREFORDSHIRE

Paul and Jackie Gardner (right) met originally over their enthusiasm for insect-eating plants.

The pitcher plant (opposite), a native of the Carolinas, is elegant and deadly.

Guy: Growing plants that eat little flies is fairly strange. How did you find the reaction at shows?

Paul Gardner: Well, people just come up with a look of amazement on their faces. Then you show them how they work and they just want the whole stand ... they get hooked.

Guy: Or trapped!

Paul Gardner started his horticultural career growing heathers and selling them wholesale. By 1987 heathers were out of fashion and he was looking for a new direction when he saw a carnivorous plant nursery up for sale near Frome in Somerset. Carnivorous plants are unique. There are between 450 and 500 species, all of which trap and digest small creatures ranging from protozoa to crustacea, spiders, small amphibians and even very small mammals. They grow into weird and fantastic shapes and have incredibly beautiful colours. Many of them are native to the Carolinas in America.

Paul met his wife Jackie at a plant sale in Swansea. It was the strange plants on his stand that attracted her first but, as Paul says, things went on from there and the relationship 'blossomed like a plant'. Jackie and her five children came to join him in Somerset and she became a valuable assistant at the shows: 'Because she was so good at designing with colours. She was a hairdresser, you see, and colour was very important. So, she was a very good designer and a very good saleswoman. Yes, we had a marvellous common denominator with the plants.' The children soon got involved, too. They loved showing customers how the different plants worked. 'We'd sometimes like to feed the children to the plants,' admits Paul, 'but on the whole they are pretty good.'

Surely the most spectacular of all carnivorous plants is the Venus flytrap, *Dionaea muscipula*, described by Charles Darwin as 'one of the most wonderful plants in the world'. It is extraordinary to see it trap and then slowly digest house flies, wasps, bluebottles and whitefly. It is not difficult to grow. It will thrive on a warm, sunny windowsill provided it is given plenty of rainwater. Tap water is too alkaline for it.

Paul has established the National Collection of Sarraceniaceae, or pitcher plants. It is just part of his and Jackie's extraordinary collection of insect-eating plants. ▼

The Tree Cathedral

Horse chestnuts (above) are the two *allées* forming the transepts.

The cathedral nave (opposite) is an avenue of lime trees.

Mrs Pam Ward: I think we enjoy it as much on a quiet summer's evening as we do when we come to a service. But we are very lucky, as are a lot of the locals who enjoy it, because you just feel there are so many things in heaven and on earth. We say 'all creatures great and small and so many things and the Lord God made them all' but here it all is, and everything else too.

In 1930 Major E. K. Blythe was returning from a holiday on the Isle of Man with his wife. They broke the journey by visiting the new Anglican cathedral in Liverpool, designed by Sir Giles Gilbert Scott. The Major was deeply affected by what he saw.

Although the First World War had been over for more than a decade, Major Blythe had always wanted to make a memorial to his friends John Burnett, Arthur Bailey and Francis Holland, who had been killed right at the end of the war. Perhaps the sight of Liverpool Cathedral reminded him of Lord Tennyson's famous words:

Speak no more of his renown.
Lay your earthly fancies down,
And in the vast cathedral leave him.
God accept him, Christ receive him.
Lord Tennyson, 'Christ Triumphans'.

By the time they reached Little Chapel Farm in Whipsnade, the house that he had bought three years earlier, the Major had decided to create a cathedral out of trees as a memorial to his friends. With the help of Alan Branson he managed to complete the planting by 1939. They used lime trees to make the pillars of the nave and a semicircle of silver birch backed by a taller yew hedge for the chancel. Horse chestnut trees were planted to mark the north and south transepts and the Christmas Chapel was, of course, made from Norwegian spruce. The Summer Chapel had pillars of whitebeam and the Lady Chapel was planted in Atlantic cedar.

During the Second World War the Tree Cathedral became very overgrown, but Major Blythe, having enlisted the help of Gerald Walsham, continued to work on it until his death in 1969. After the Major's death the site was given to the National Trust and it is cared for by trustees.

The trustees work very hard to maintain the cathedral so that it continues to reflect Major Blythe's original vision. At the centre of the structure there is a natural dew pond which is used by many animals, including deer, during the summer. The trustees have had to repuddle the pond twice recently. They also keep the main areas clear of brambles and unwanted saplings.

The Cathedral is open 365 days a year and during the summer it is often used for services. To walk through the Tree Cathedral, even when it is empty, is to be reminded of matters spiritual in an increasingly cynical world. ▼

Farm Follies

SOUTH MOLTON, DEVON

The Radfords (below) stand behind the redesigned remains of tractors once ridden by Bob himself.

A view across the Radfords' garden (opposite) to the fertile Devonian fields beyond.

Mr and Mrs Radford both come from Devonshire farming families and have some antipathy to anything happening beyond the county border. Mr Radford inherited 120 hectares (300 acres) from his father and he worked the land until about ten years ago, when he was obliged to give up farming for health reasons.

The Radfords sold the farmhouse and about 80 hectares (200 acres). In 1990 they built a new house on a windswept field. Two years later they decided to think about the garden. The rubble from the drive was pushed away from the house to form a level route to a new barn and garage. A large hole

on the site was the inspiration for a pond below the slope. This was the first step in creating the water garden close to the house. The water now appears to seep from a rock and flow down through a series of small pools.

A lawn was made in front of the house and trees were planted around the water feature, but soon the Radfords' energies sought a greater outlet. They looked at the surrounding fields and the landscape beyond – a scattering of hedges and meadows, with plenty of changing levels and plays of light. It was all too tempting. The sheep were banned from the 0.8 hectares (2 acres) closest to the house and a belt of trees was planted in an attempt to solve a serious wind problem. Now that the space was prepared, decisions had to be made about what to put in this extension of the garden. Their inspiration came from an amazing collection of old agricultural machinery in their barns, which they realised had the potential to be contemporary sculptures.

One such creation is made from five tiers of wheels welded together like metal acrobats. Because of their great age, some of the wheels are greenish in colour, some are brown and others almost silver. Behind them a hedge about 2.4m (8ft) tall acts as a backdrop. Elsewhere, a job lot of eight granite gateposts has been transformed into a miniature Devonshire version of the

THEIR INSPIRATION CAME FROM AN AMAZING COLLECTION OF
OLD AGRICULTURAL MACHINERY IN THEIR BARNS, WHICH THEY REALISED
HAD THE POTENTIAL TO BE CONTEMPORARY SCULPTURES.

Avebury stone circle. It took a great deal of time and effort to get them into position because they are so cumbersome, and the JCB driver's patience was sorely tested. They still have their iron gate hangers on them as a reminder of their original function. Elsewhere, four granite stones form a table, or is it a contemporary dolmen (a prehistoric burial chamber)? The two acres have also become a mini-arboretum in which a very wide variety of trees are grown.

The Radfords' energy is infectious. They love what they are doing, and we wonder how many more acres will be incorporated into the garden before they are finally satisfied. There are wonderful views from the garden over the Crooked Oak river and Mole Valley. Two tractor seats placed on an old axle are a good place to sit and enjoy them. Bob remembers spending many a day on one of these seats, turning the hay behind horses. ▼

Eight granite gateposts (opposite) have become the Radfords' own miniature Avebury.

Trio of Gardens

ECCLES-ON-SEA, NORFOLK

Doris and Jerry Rollings in their front garden (above) on the Norfolk coast, which is a great deal quieter than their last garden under the Heathrow flight path.

Tim Foord and his neighbour, Bob Morris (opposite), admiring his collection of plants which flower so close to the North Sea.

Jerry Rollings: Across the road there's a couple of our friends. Tim, his front garden is brilliant. He starts at 4 o'clock in the morning, because he's a working man. I said to him the other day, I can't understand how you get your garden like this when you are never here. And that's what he said, 4 o'clock in the morning he starts, early light.

Eccles-on-Sea is a little village right on the Norfolk coast, protected from the North Sea by a long breakwater some 9m (30ft) high, which separates the sea and shingle from the village itself. The village contains a large caravan site and a prefab development dating from the end of the Second World War. Other houses here are of a similar simple wooden construction, and were designed as inexpensive summer homes. In this unlikely village there are three gardeners who are obsessed with different aspects of gardening.

GARDEN NUMBER ONE: DORIS & JERRY ROLLINGS

Doris and Jerry Rollings first came to Eccles-on-Sea some years ago because their son had a girlfriend living nearby. They fell in love with the place, bought a house and came to live here permanently when they retired. The home they left behind was on the Heathrow flight path. The overgrown garden and lawn in front of the house have now been swept away and the entire area to front and back is paved. There is just room for a caravan at the back, which is useful when too many children, grandchildren or great-grandchildren come to stay.

The Rollings love flowers and they have learned about the plants that will bloom in the strong, salt-laden winds off the North Sea. Almost all of their plants are grown in pots. They are both involved in choosing them, but Doris sulks if she can't have asters. Fuchsias are another favourite, and there is also an echium with a 2m (7ft) flower stalk. Jerry likes geraniums and they both love lilies. As a permanent display in the front part of the garden they have some old washtubs, one rigged as a fountain, a mangle, blue and white bread bins, cider jugs and various enamelled advertisement signs which include Pears' Soap, Reckitt's Blue and Bird's Custard. In the garden at the back there is a pool. It is here that Jerry and Doris sit to admire their garden when they have a moment's peace from the visits of their many offspring.

GARDEN NUMBER TWO: TIM FOORD

Tim Foord is just up the road from the Rollings and he is obsessed with bedding plants. A trellis covered with honeysuckle

does something to protect the plants in his front garden from the wind. He has gardened his plot for about four years. There is a circular bed with a path around it in the middle of the garden and in one corner there is a rockery devoted to alpines. In order to contain the soil, Foord has edged the bed with red bricks. He digs in a lot of compost, which encourages the plants to thrive in these challenging conditions.

One side of the garden is marked by a line of teasels which help to divert the wind and attract the birds. Below them grow self-seeded foxgloves and marigolds. Among Tim Foord's favourite flowers are sweet peas, anemones, periwinkles, the passion flower, which seems to love the climate, and jasmine. He also has roses, arbutus, eucalyptus and choisya. He gets up at dawn to look after the garden before going to work.

GARDEN NUMBER THREE: BOB MORRIS & ROY SCANNELL

Bob Morris lives next door to Tim Foord. Morris and his friend Roy Scannell have a garden of sub-tropical exotics and much else. These plants are screened from the winds by a tall hedge of vigorous pink lavatera. When we arrived Morris had just planted another tree-fern, a *Dicksonia antarctica*, indigenous to New Zealand and Australia. The tree-fern is

unique and fascinating in that both vigorous roots and frond shoots are encased in the tough, fibrous tree trunk. Tree-ferns do not mind salty air but they need protection if the temperature falls below freezing.

It is almost impossible to find a way through this garden which is 9m x 6m (30ft x 20ft). It is filled to overflowing with sub-tropical plant material, such as eucalyptus, echium, an unexpected gunnera, a banana tree, phormiums, achillea, *Melianthus major* and *Leucadendron argenteum*. Just to remind us that we are actually in the English county of Norfolk, there is one hollyhock.

Bob is helped in the garden by his friend Roy, and they are always trying to find more sub-tropical plants that will grow at Eccles-on-Sea. Their problem is, of course, one of limited space. Many of the plants grow to 3m (10ft). They both look longingly at the empty garden next door; it must be their *horror vaccuii* syndrome. Meanwhile they spend a great deal of time looking after their sub-tropical paradise, only 180m (200yds) away from the North Sea. ▼

Bob Morris and Roy Scannell (opposite) at night peering through the palm tree in their unusual jungle garden occasionally harassed by the winds blowing down from Siberia.

Flag Garden

BROUGHTON, LANARKSHIRE, SCOTLAND

The ardent Scottish nationalist, Tom Shearer, in front of his favourite flag, the Cross of St Andrew, planted up with 650 violas.

Tom Shearer: I'm very keen on having plants that will keep flowering all the time. You'll not see any American marigolds here ...

Gordon: Whaddya mean?

Tom Shearer: They are no use here.

Gordon: They probably don't want to travel anyway. A lot of Americans don't want to travel, they'd rather go to Disneyland.

Broughton is a small village of attractive cottages in a fold of the Pentland Hills. It lies about 50 km (30 miles) due south of Edinburgh. For centuries it had a coaching inn and there are records stating that the Highland Army of Bonnie Prince Charlie dropped in during the November of 1795 and demanded provisions from the houses in the village.

Tom Shearer bought Beechgrove with 2.8 hectares (7 acres) for £3,000 in 1960. There was a paved area to one side of the house and a very large beech tree dominated the garden. Tom immediately removed the paving and the tree, leaving an empty brown space. He then concocted a mixture of 24D/245T and Amino Triasol. 'I put them all together,' he told us, 'although they weren't supposed to be mixed. That was all the chemicals available at the time.' He sprayed the garden throughout the summer with this deadly cocktail and by the autumn there wasn't a single weed left. 'It was bare earth and I've never had a perennial weed since, in forty years.' Despite hints that he might offend viewers committed to organic cultivation, Tom was unrepentant, announcing proudly: 'I use every chemical available to mankind.'

In 1961 the front garden area was put down to grass. The chemical warfare continued. 'I put half a hundredweight of worm killer on that,' he said. The lawn is cut to half an inch during the growing season, usually three times a week, but sometimes every 24 hours. Each mowing takes exactly 7 minutes and 40 seconds. He never removes the grass cuttings. The result is a sheet of smooth, green, ultra-suede nap.

Shearer's annual bedding display has become famous. What with tour buses and cars, he has calculated that 100,000 people visit his garden each year. 'I used to let them in,' he told us, 'but there would be too many now and they'd leave the lawn like a rugby field.' Last year he collected £1,500 for charity in an old milk tin.

Shearer describes himself as 'a rabid Scottish Nationalist' and this year the centrepiece of the display is the saltire flag of St Andrew, the patron saint of Scotland. The blue part is planted in the extremely pretty Viola 'Maggie Mott' and the two white stripes are the Viola cornuta alba. Out of the 5,000 bedding plants which he grows himself each year, about 650 are used to make up the flag.

The garden is in a frost pocket. Shearer told us that only three weeks earlier, in mid-July, he was lying in bed in the middle of the night when his nose began to twitch. 'My nose always twitches when I'm in bed and it's frosty outside.' He got up, scraped the ice off the cold frames and went back to bed when he saw that the sky was beginning to cloud over. He knew that the temperature would rise under the blanket of cloud, saving his poor plants. On other occasions he has stayed up the entire night, watering the plants to prevent the frost settling on them. On these occasions a bottle of malt whisky stands on the windowsill of the house, to be used as his own form of anti-freeze.

The hedge that Shearer has planted around the boundary has done something to protect the garden from the strong south-westerly winds. It allows him to grow a much wider range of plants than is usually possible in the area. However, he is very firm with his plants. 'I only grow plants that grow like weeds,' he told us. 'If they are not thriving they are thrown out. An awful lot of gardeners spend their time trying to grow something just because it comes from Timbuktu. Well, in my opinion it should go back there. I only grow things that luxuriate in this climate.'

On a slope above the road Shearer has installed a small arboretum together with a collection of fruit trees, a strawberry patch and unusual hedges of delicious golden dessert gooseberries from the old walled garden of a nearby estate. These and many of the other well-established plants in his garden came from cuttings that he has collected on his rounds as a horticultural adviser. So, it's all true what we say in England about the canny Scots …

The great annual border display which helps attract the remarkable figure of 100,000 viewers; they come by the bus-load.

Clematis Garden

AYLESBURY, BUCKINGHAMSHIRE

Clematis at the top is
C. 'Kathleen Dunford' (right)
and the one at the bottom is
Clematis viticella 'Etoile Violette'.

The photographer caught Jackie
and Haydn Goodair mid-task
(opposite), for the clematis
obsessive's work is never done.

The Goodairs bought their house in Aylesbury nine years ago. They didn't tackle the garden, a plot 15m (50ft) wide and 36m (120ft) long, until they had been in the house for a year. There were two cherry trees and two maples at the bottom of it, lots of brambles and three changes of level. The cherry nearest the house had to be felled to make way for a conservatory. The second level of the garden is in full sun, and this is where most of the new planting was done. The third level, on slightly higher ground at the back of the garden, is the site of a greenhouse, potting sheds and a series of arches. There is no direct view down the garden, and this draws one on to explore.

The garden reflects Jackie's obsession with clematis and, eight years on, we think that she has created clematis heaven. It all started with a *Clematis montana* that she grew in the garden of her previous home. She brought it with her to the new garden – quite an achievement as their long and delicate root structure can make clematis hard to move. Jackie now has 126 different varieties, chosen to ensure that something will be in flower throughout the year. As she says, 'You start the year with *C. armandii*, which is evergreen and full of scent ... and you just go on and on, and when there isn't anything left you've got wonderful seed heads ... '

Clematis prefer to have warm feet and cool faces. This is not always possible, but Jackie has been extremely clever in organising herbaceous plant material to grow around the roots of her clematis specimens. They are greedy feeders and she gives them tomato fertiliser from the start of the season, as well as blood, fish and bone, plenty of water and a generous mulch. Jackie has also mastered the art of growing clematis in pots. We saw both *C. integra* and *C.* 'Josephine Hill' flourishing in pots placed near to the conservatory.

Jackie has travelled the length and breadth of the country in order to build up her collection, and she is especially fond of two clematis specialists, Barry Fretwell and Jim Fisk. She thinks that her obsession probably

THE GARDEN REFLECTS JACKIE'S OBSESSION WITH CLEMATIS AND,
EIGHT YEARS ON, WE THINK THAT SHE HAS CREATED CLEMATIS HEAVEN.

The Clematis Garden (opposite) is full of both design and plant surprises; it is a wonderland of verticals for climbers.

took root when she first saw Jim Fisk's stand at Chelsea. She was simply amazed by the variety of colour and form. She is not sure exactly how many varieties of clematis there are altogether, but she thinks that one day she and Haydn may have to move house so that they can expand their collection even further in a larger garden.

Jackie is a terrific plantswoman who describes herself as 'a plantaholic'. She is perpetually struggling to find room for just one more plant in the garden. New clematis varieties are always being bred and, as she says, 'You just want them all!' She has developed brilliant ways of combining clematis with other plants. We were particularly struck by a lovely combination of various tones of purpley-reds for which she used a sport of *Clematis* 'Nellie Moser', the dark velvety rose 'Reine des Violettes' and the stunning claret-coloured poppy *Papaver* 'Patty's Plum'; the last named after Patty Marrow, that wonderful plantswoman in Somerset.

It is only by walking through the garden that one experiences how subtly the plant material has been used and the attention that has been paid to different colours, heights and leaf shapes. Jackie says the main colours in the garden, including the clematis, are pinks, blues and whites, but she does accept the need for an occasional glimpse of yellow or orange. ▼

Littlethorpe Potteries

PARK HILL GRANGE, LITTLETHORPE, YORKSHIRE

In 1901 there were 100 workers at the potteries, and now there is only Roly Curtis (above), a third-generation master potter.

Roly Curtis pushes a bogie (opposite) a couple of hundred feet from the ancient clay pit to the pottery – uphill all the way!

Roly Curtis: You have to have a feel for it. You could sit and watch me all day, but you wouldn't be able to do it. It takes years to learn to make the big pots.

Littlethorpe Pottery may not be the oldest in the country. It is the 'oldest working pottery' or the oldest pottery that mines its own clay. In the early 1900s the pottery came into the Curtis family and Roly and Christine Curtis are the third generation to continue in the family tradition.

The pottery was built on the site because there is a deposit of alluvial clay only 1.2m (4ft) below the top soil. In places it is 14m (48ft) deep. The clay deposit is probably 10–20,000 years old, which is quite young in comparison to other geological strata in Yorkshire.

Between the pottery building and the clay deposits there are twin iron rails on which a bogie, or cart, runs. Curtis digs the clay as needed and pushes the bogie from the clay deposit, across a small stream, up the few hundred feet of slope to the yard to prepare the clay. When he is making big pots, he needs up to 3 tonnes (3 tons) of clay each week. This means five trips with the bogie. In the experienced hands of Curtis, a wet lump of clay on the wheel is transformed into a rounded, beautiful pot in less than five minutes.

When the Curtis family first bought the pottery they employed a hundred people to produce bricks, roof and floor tiles and land drains. By the time Roly decided to follow in the family tradition – he had started out as an industrial chemist – he succeeded his father as the sole worker in the pottery. Most of the other potteries in the area had already gone out of business because of the advent of plastics in the 1950s.

Roly still uses the nineteenth-century coal furnace that heats his pots to 1,000 degrees C. The kiln uses 10 tonnes (10 tons) of coal over a thirty-six-hour period. The porous, high-fired clay pots are ideal for growing plants.

All Curtis' pots are made on a rotary wheel. He makes pots for hostas, box bushes, agapanthus lilies, forcing pots for rhubarb and sea kale and long toms in three different sizes. It might be thought that these last pots were for growing tomatoes, but they are not. They can be used to bring on any kind of plant.

There is a courtyard between the pottery and the shop. Here some of the pots are planted up. The biggest ones hold ornamental bay trees and other topiary, while the smaller ones are planted with a wide variety of herbs, geraniums and summer annuals. Littlethorpe is the only pottery of its kind left in Yorkshire. A lot of people know about it and on the open day this year there were more than 2,000 visitors. ▼

A collection of Curtis' pots, which more knowledgeable gardeners prefer to the ubiquitous plastic.

Succulent Garden

PENRYN, CORNWALL

A small multicoloured wall (above) inspired by Gaudí's Parque Güell in Barcelona.

Oliver Bennett looks out (opposite) on his giant echiums, more than twice his height.

Sometimes, size has everything to do with it. Oliver Bennett, who has made a sub-tropical garden at the back of his house in the middle of Penryn, must be 1.9m (6ft 4in) tall, the average height of an echium. It has taken three years for Bennett's echiums to defy average growth records and produce growth spikes 4.2m (14ft) high. He has grown three specimens in a garden only 3.6m (12ft) wide and 12m (40ft) long.

Bennett trained as a tree surgeon and then worked with a nursery specialising in hardy exotics. One of their projects involved the creation of a vast bank of sub-tropical plants and Bennett became hooked on cacti and succulents, which flourish in Cornwall's mild climate. On the rare occasions that the temperature falls below zero, Bennett wraps the sub-tropical plants in horticultural fleece. To date he has been very fortunate and in three years he has created an amazing sub-tropical jungle in his narrow, steeply sloping town garden.

When Bennett first arrived he had to deal with the slope up from the kitchen, a senseless grassy patch, and a great deal of rubble. Now there is a paved area immediately outside the kitchen and the garden rises in three levels. All the rubble was used to improve the drainage throughout the garden. This was essential because most sub-tropical plants need excellent drainage. A path and steps carry you from one level to another, but the route is never direct. This is a deliberate feature, ensuring that the whole garden can never be seen at once. The visitor is encouraged to explore, hopefully avoiding the needle-sharp tips of some very large variegated agave. These can be painful if you get within pricking distance. Bennett has thoughtfully provided wine cork guards on the spikes nearest the main path.

We are familiar with the agave or aloe from our travels in Mexico. It is a very important plant there, and every part of it is used. The dried fibre is woven into shawls, serapes and bags. It is also the source of a highly beneficial emollient and an ingredient of

Part of this collection of 160 succulents (opposite) need cosseting in agricultural fleece on the very occasional frosty night in Cornwall.

tequila, that powerful Mexican firewater.

A small water feature at the top of the garden is bounded by a low retaining wall decorated with a mosaic made from sea-washed terracotta shards and broken mirrors. The random patterns, reminiscent of Gaudí's Parque Güell in Barcelona, were inspired by a poster brought back for Bennett from Spain by his girlfriend. The pool area has been organised to provide moisture and shade for any plants that need it.

As well as the seventy or eighty species of succulent and cacti that Bennett grows, the garden contains a very wide range of other plant material, including a *Melianthus major* against the wall which is now more than 4m (13ft) high. In this very small area he grows approximately 160 different species and he is always adding to his collection. The garden requires constant work, even during the winter months, and he applies fish, blood and bone meal at monthly intervals.

As he sits in his kitchen, in winter or summer, Bennett can look out at his garden and be transported to warmer places. 'This is my little piece of paradise,' he says 'and it certainly beats mowing the lawn on a Sunday afternoon.' ▼

Boyce's Nursery

SHILLINGFORD ST GEORGE, DEVON

Our favourite hanging basket (above), planted up with just one type of plant – a pretty blue lobelia.

Tim and Simon Boyce (opposite) with a few of the 4,000 hanging baskets they produce each year.

Tim Boyce: I grow the plants for Simon to use in the planting up. He's like a basket battery hen. We supply the fodder and he lays all these baskets.

Tim and Simon Boyce are the proprietors of Boyce's, a company that makes up and sells approximately 4,000 hanging baskets each year. They sell a range of annual and perennial plant material, either for hanging baskets or for planting in pots and other containers. In contrast to the usual practice, the two sons employ their parents.

At a demonstration table in the shop, Simon explained how you fill a hanging basket. The first choice to be made was between a plastic or a wire basket – the Boyces generally prefer wire. The basket is lined with dry sphagnum moss, the mossy side being placed against the wire frame. This is then dampened, so that it is just moist to the touch. A fine black plastic liner is inserted, followed by a peat-based compost to which some slow-release fertiliser is added along with a moisture enhancer. So long as the basket is kept wet, the fertiliser will help the roots of the plant to grow as it expands. The plastic is then trimmed just below the edge of the basket and it is ready for planting.

A 35cm (14in) basket takes eight plants to start with. Simon Boyce showed us how to push the plants through the lining from the inside of the basket. This protects the roots, though a leaf or two may be lost in the process. A little more compost may be needed to fill the basket right up, although the compost should not be too firm. Two plants are put in the centre and a further eight are added around them. Depending on their size, it may be necessary to add a further circle of eight more plants, making twenty-six plants in all. Thereafter, the basket needs watering twice a week and feeding once a month. With care, it should last from May to September and sometimes even until Christmas.

Hanging baskets are traditionally associated with pubs and hotels. They are also popular with municipal authorities, who use them to brighten up the streets. We have to admit that hanging baskets drive us up the wall. However, for a more contemporary look the Brothers Boyce fill some of their baskets with a single species in only one colour. We thought that these single-colour baskets were a great improvement on the traditional look. It's nothing to do with being 'good taste' designers; they just read much simpler and better than the multicoloured ones, and we quite liked them. ▼

Malleny Garden

BALERNO, LOTHIAN, SCOTLAND

Main path edged by symmetrical rows of vegetables (below) chosen for aesthetic reasons as well as practical use.

On the left (opposite) is a wigwam with vigorous runner beans and in the middle another covered in sweet peas, both sharing the common name Painted Lady.

Guy: I can't think why we are going to see somebody who grows bonsais.

Gordon: Well, I can, because I happen to like them. I know they are highly artificial, but they are so artful.

Guy: They may be artful, but they have nothing to do with gardens and nothing to do with landscape.

Gordon: Yes, they do! They are miniature trees.

As well as being the home of the Scottish National Bonsai Collection, Malleny House, near Edinburgh, has a remarkable vegetable garden designed and maintained by Philip Deacon. The principle behind the design is that appearance should be just as important as the flavour of the different crops. The vegetables are enclosed by a high wall which provides security and protection from the wind. The planting is extremely carefully planned to provide interest throughout the year. The layout was inspired by a French potager. What a contrast it makes to all those dreary, regimented back gardens seen from train windows all over the country: row upon row of rotting Brussels sprouts. Perhaps the veg patch is just a chance for 'im to get away from 'er indoors? At Malleny, the formal design is as pretty as a picture, for Deacon has interplanted the vegetables with flowers, some of which are edible, like the delicious nasturtium.

Deacon couldn't tell us how many different types of vegetables he grew, but he suspected it was between forty and fifty. The only ones that will not grow are carrots, parsnips and bulb fennel, because of the shallowness of the soil. The routine for feeding the soil is organic, mainly depending upon the regular maintenance of some adjacent compost heaps. Along one of the rows there were some wire cages which Deacon calls topiary balls. Unusually, he was growing peas up and around them. They also make a formal architectural decoration for the vegetable garden in spring and early summer. On the other side there were some wigwam climbing frames covered in runner beans.

In an adjacent bed, partly on account of their colour and partly their use, both real and alleged, are some herbs. These include Good King Henry (*Chenopodium bonus-henricus*), much used in salads during the seventeenth century. Its young shoots were seen as an alternative to asparagus. This was one of the many 'sallett' herbs that we grew when we had Tumblers Bottom Herb Farm. We found it as tasteless then as we do now. Deacon was also growing great pots of madder (*Rubia tinctorum*). Its roots have been used for millennia as the source of a red dye.

In early August, Malleny was looking as beautiful as any vegetable garden we have ever seen. This was due to careful planning. The leaf pattern of each bed complemented its neighbour, while contrasting with the annual flowers grown among the vegetables. The garden had an ordered, relaxed quality without that overwrought, tense regimentation that we have seen in so many other formal British potagers, often designed by those cut-glass-accented granny gardeners. The success of the garden may in part be due to the fact that it is purely decorative. The seventeenth-century house and garden were presented to the National Trust for Scotland in 1968. The only people who ever use any vegetables are Deacon and his assistant gardener. These they pluck with much care so that the overall effect is not disturbed.

The decline in very large vegetable gardens is mainly due to the amount of maintenance that they demand throughout the year. As maintenance is the main consideration when designing a garden, choices have to be made between decorative flowers, shrubs and the more practical areas of the garden.

When we asked Philip about the visitors who come to Malleny he told us that 'Some come for the bonsai, some for the roses, but most people come here because it's peaceful.' The tranquillity of Malleny is certainly noticeable. The shrub roses represent one of the largest collections in Britain and it draws in visitors from all over the world.

The Scottish National Bonsai Collection is Malleny's other treasure. It is tucked away in a corner of the gardens in one of the old greenhouses and, for the sake of security, it is locked into a mesh cage. Our personal attitudes to the collection were certainly divided. Guy believes that 'Japanese things are fine in Japan, but they look out of place anywhere else in the world.' Gordon, however, was impressed by the skill demonstrated by the two dozen carers appointed by the Scottish Bonsai Association, whose job it is to look after development and maintenance of the exquisite miniature trees. ▼

High security (opposite) necessitates caging the Scottish National Bonsai Collection.

Priorwood Garden

MELROSE, BORDERS, SCOTLAND

Head Gardener Andrew Leitch and Property Manager Cathy Ross (above) holding bunches of flowers about to be dried at Priorwood Gardens.

The major herbaceous border (opposite) is planted both to be beautiful during the summer and to provide material for drying.

Guy: I have been amazed by the amount of time and effort that people lavish on their gardens.

Gordon: But isn't that part of the peculiar British obsession with gardens?

Guy: So, our American friend is beginning to realise why we are such a great nation of gardeners!

Gordon: Do you have a flag that you can wave? I am so good humoured, so objective. Americans have a breadth of vision that allows them to understand you Brits, with all your foibles and eccentricities.

Priorwood Garden, which has belonged to the National Trust for Scotland since 1974, was originally part of the precinct of Melrose Abbey. Almost as soon as the Trust took it over, a group of enthusiastic volunteers started drying and selling flowers to help defray the costs of running the garden. Since 1990 various new facilities have been built so that flowers and plants can be both dried and displayed, contributing greatly to the experience of visiting the gardens.

Very close to the entrance are two major beds, one for cultivating herbaceous plants and the other for growing annual plants, both types being chosen to remain both colourful and attractive when dried. The herbaceous border includes a wide range of achillea, astrantia, monarda, peonies, eryngium and euphorbia along with *Echinops ritro* 'Veitch's Blue' and *Gypsophila paniculata* 'Bristol Fairy'. The annual beds include amaranthus, calendula, helipterum, helichrysum, poppies and salvias. There is also a herb garden, and more recently a grass garden which lists seventeen different sorts of grasses, adding to the scale and variety of plant material which can be dried.

In high summer the herbaceous border, which is about 15m (50ft) long, is one of the finest we have ever seen. This year it was filled with an enchanting range of yellow and golden flowers. The annual beds were equally attractive and it became clear that although

FLOWERS SHOULD NEVER BE BUNCHED TOGETHER
AS PEOPLE SO OFTEN DO IN THEIR KITCHENS.
THIS LEADS TO THE FLOWERS AROUND THE EDGE OF THE BUNCH
DRYING TOO QUICKLY AND THOSE IN THE MIDDLE DECAYING.

A corner of the garden (below) where seventeen species of grasses are grown, which are wonderful and very decorative.

Bunches of thistles, amaranthus and different-coloured daisies (opposite) prepared for air drying.

the flowers were chosen for drying, the plant combinations also produced very satisfactory and colourful displays for a long time during the growing year.

There are basically two ways to dry flowers. In one method the flower heads are removed from the stems and put into trays of sand. The sand is combined with a drying agent and the flowers are then very carefully and completely buried in the sand. This drying process takes about four weeks. The other way is to take the longer-stemmed flowers and hang them individually in a dry dark place where the temperature is maintained at about 80 degrees. Priorwood has a purpose-built drying room.

Flowers should never be bunched together as people so often do in their kitchens.

This leads to the flowers around the edge of the bunch drying too quickly and those in the middle decaying. The decay then spreads to the rest of the stems. So, when you see those photographs of so-called 'country kitchens' with dried flowers hanging from the ceiling, bear in mind that they are probably midway through the rotting process! Up to ten volunteers work in the drying and display areas at Priorwood for nine months of the year. During January, February and March the garden is closed.

The range of dried flowers and grasses displayed and sold at Priorwood is very wide. They also offer a service to brides, who can have their wedding bouquets dried and preserved, provided the flowers are suitable, for the cost of approximately £25. ▼

Gardens Contemporary

Aluminium and acrylic pyramids, fibreoptic lighting, formalised water and rigorous minimalist planting make a superb twenty-first-century design.

There has been an explosion of contemporary gardens all over Britain. When we were planning the series with the BBC, we said that we wanted at least one example of contemporary design in each episode. In the event, our research revealed so many examples that most episodes have at least two gardens in this category.

Great Britain has led the world in the design of the private garden for centuries. The pattern continues to this day. Owners are looking at their 'space outside' with new eyes, and are having revolutionary contemporary ideas about what they want to see in it. These new areas are often part of a larger, horticulturally inspired garden. They pull part of the traditional garden into the new millennium.

Garden owners are recognising that any material and any plant species in any combination can be used. Steel, aluminium, glass, which can be clear, shot-blasted or acid-etched, water, which can be calm, agitated or used as a film over a stone, and lighting, both low-voltage and fibreoptic. Spotlights can be dimmed and directed. Fibreoptics can be used in many dazzling conformations, embroidering the ground, as myriad points in a pool or bathing a focal point at the end of a path. All of these 'high-tech' props can be used as part of the transformation of the garden landscape into something that is truly expressive of contemporary life.

Yorkshire Sculpture Park

WEST BRETTON, YORKSHIRE

Sol LeWitt's conceptual sculpture, *123454321* (above), has caused much controversy among the visitors.

The root plate of a fallen 250-year-old beech (opposite) was transmuted into a sculpture, *Homage to Mondrian*, by Polish sculptor Joanna Przybyla.

The Yorkshire Sculpture Park was founded in 1977 as Britain's first permanent sculpture park. It shares the landscape with a grand eighteenth-century stately home, Bretton Hall, now a college of the nearby University of Leeds. The estate covers 240 hectares (600 acres) and the sculpture park uses about 120 hectares (300 acres) of them. The facilities include two indoor galleries and nine distinct open-air spaces for changing exhibitions and projects. The work of many major British sculptors is displayed, including that of Elisabeth Frink, Sir Anthony Caro, Lynn Chadwick, Barbara Hepworth, Sir Eduardo Paolozzi and David Nash.

The park has an 'Access' sculpture trail, designed so that it can easily be used by people pushing prams or using wheelchairs. Visitors are invited to touch and enjoy the sculptures exhibited outside, so that they can heighten their appreciation through the use of their five senses. The sculptures shown in the galleries, however, are off-limits. At least half of the artists on show in the temporary exhibitions and projects are international: Gió Pomodoro, Italy; Igor Mitoraj, Italy/Poland; Sol LeWitt and Richard Serra, United States. Both Pomodoro and Serra are known for their work in metal, so the pieces here in Yorkshire are an exception, being in Portland stone and marble.

Paths inside the sculpture park lead away from the university buildings, towards the lake and the river and into the woods beyond. Walking the grounds at Bretton Hall is a wonderful adventure, for one never knows what sculptures one may find, or where. Sculpture exhibitions are also staged below a considerable run of nineteenth-century garden outbuildings and a beautifully curved brick wall which formed part of the old walled garden and originally supported a spectacular range of nineteenth-century glasshouses.

There is a grand terrace below the outbuildings, and the inevitable country-house herbaceous border. In the middle of the terrace is a large metal sculpture by Antony Gormley. It is about 4.5m (15ft) high and made up of a series of disjointed limbs which enhance the three-dimensional effect. Culture vulture scores by the curious gardeners: Taylor 0, but Cooper 7. Gormley has also made *The Angel of the North*,

ART THAT EMPHASISES CONTENT (SUCH AS MINE) CANNOT BE SEEN OR
UNDERSTOOD IN A CONTEXT OF FORM.
THIS IS A LARGE AND CRUCIAL DIFFERENCE. IT CANNOT BE SAID THAT WHAT
LOOKS ALIKE IS ALIKE. IF ONE WISHES TO UNDERSTAND THE ART
OF OUR TIME ONE MUST GO BEYOND APPEARANCE.

Sol LeWitt

Rhizome Three (opposite), a bronze contemporary sculpture by Antony Gormley, contrasts with the grand nineteenth-century formal terrace.

that huge, controversial sculpture outside Gateshead.

Near to the river is *Homage to Mondrian* by Polish artist Joanna Przybyla. It is a massive installation made in 1995 from a 250-year-old storm-damaged beech. The root plate has a diameter of 3.6m (12ft). Przybyla has stabilised it with an uneven grid of metal staples which are a direct homage to Piet Mondrian, the great abstract painter. The dramatic sculpture has begun to slowly decay back into the landscape; meanwhile it serves as a wonderful climbing frame for more adventurous children.

Nearby is a sculpture by Sol LeWitt called 123454321. It is made out of concrete blocks arranged in five steps. The structure is three blocks wide. It is a superb example of conceptual minimalism based on simple numerical systems and serial progressions. It is very simple and some people, like Gordon Taylor, love it. Others, like Guy Cooper, ask, 'What is this detritus left over from a building site?'

The park is a fascinating setting for the sculptures. Visitors may love them or hate them, but they will not forget them and that is surely one of the main objectives of the Yorkshire Sculpture Park. A visit to the sculpture park can be combined with a trip to Bretton Country Park next door, which has a changing display of magnificent sculptures by the Yorkshire-born Sir Henry Moore. ▼

Kilcot

KILCOT, GLOUCESTERSHIRE

Shock and pleasure: after walking through a traditional cottage garden, there are abstract twentieth-century sculptures of *yin* and *yang* (above).

Paul Cooper has designed these most pleasing verticals (opposite) based on Dürer's theory of the Golden Section.

Gordon: Think of the insides of people's houses. They'll be painted white, a trendy cheese grater in the kitchen and an Andy Warhol print on the wall. Fax machines, mobiles, computers, they are all there, inside the house. But when they get to the garden door, what happens?

Guy: You're back in the nineteenth century.

Gordon: Exactly, and usually one of the mothers-in-law is brought in to advise. She'll say, 'Oh dears, you don't really want to be controversial,' and that will be it.

Guy: But that's all changing now, isn't it?

Ken and Ann Allen bought their Gloucestershire home in 1975, when the house was derelict and the garden a wilderness. Over the years they have worked with Paul Cooper, one of Britain's leading contemporary garden designers, to transform the site into an experimental space where they could explore contemporary ideas. As Ken told us, Paul Cooper got them started, '... and once the ball's rolling it's the natural energy. You start to realise that in a wonderful, rural location like this, you can still bring contemporary design into your life space. To come home and feel the new as well as the natural is a great feeling.'

Paul Cooper's real contribution to the garden was to give them a 'narrative'. 'The concept of a garden being designed around a narrative was really valuable to me,' Ken told

us. 'It's something you can talk about and understand.' In the case of this garden, the narrative was a complex one: 'It was based on a picture, based on the world, it was based on the river of life, a mother, a goddess, the source of life. Out of this structure came modern shapes, modern sculptures, a modern garden.' The great thing about the garden to our minds was that, narrative or not, it works as pure design.

There is a stream separating the Allens' garden from the adjoining meadow. Willows which they have maintained and encouraged for the last twenty-five years form a living screen. A recent examination of 1 sq m (1 sq yd) of the meadow revealed forty-nine different plant species. Each spring the meadow grows as it will and is first mown in mid-August and then on a bi-weekly basis until the end of the growing season. In one corner the Allens have just erected an impressive living willow sculpture, a cupola, designed by Ewen McEwen. He has made a 4.5m (15ft) circle out of 3m (10ft) long willow cuttings which are being trained to form a 4.5m (15ft) high dome-shaped structure. Inside there will be a living willow seat where you will be able to look through an open 'window' to the meadow and the lake beyond.

To the right of the cottage door is an area called *La Source* designed by Paul Cooper. It is inspired by the Ingres painting entitled

Spring. Paul Cooper's interpretation consists of a stylised trellis sculpture showing a goddess pouring water from a clay pitcher. The water, the source of life, is represented by slates laid on edge. The twists and turns of the water are built into the slate as it flows over a boulder and creates a rill, finally cascading into a genuine pool where golden orfe swim. Overhead are two shiny, arching aluminium pipe sections which are in balance, representing the *yin* and *yang*, the male and female, with weights that touch the water's surface as the poles move.

Beyond this garden and the house is the Conversations Garden, also designed by Paul Cooper. Once again Paul has created a narrative structure and this time the subject is theatre. Timber decking suggests the 'boards'. Two topiary figures represent the actors. They are talking to each other and, as Ken says, 'There is obviously a lot of intrigue going on. Whether they are talking about us or starting a romance, we don't know.' When the Allens have a party, the guests come out into the garden with their drinks and chat alongside the sculptures.

Between *La Source* and the Conversations Garden, there is the Meditation Garden, designed by another leading contemporary garden designer, Judy Toll. This is a square enclosure planted with yew. On one side is a bronze Buddha set in beautiful, calming green and white planting. The centre of the garden is formed from a large square of raised wooden decking in which is enclosed a contrasting circle. Dark and light timbers are used to emphasise the circle in the square, and the circle is reflected again in the mirrored backdrop of the Buddha.

The Jardiniere garden next door was designed by Judy Toll in the spirit of Piet Oudolf, the Dutch naturalistic designer. The dominant colours are yellow, blue, red and burgundy. Against this background stand six metal sculptures which are Paul Cooper's interpretation of the work of Dürer. The verticals are metal components representing that artist's interpretation of the Golden Section.

The Allens' garden is always changing, partly because of their professional interest in exploring contemporary design in the garden, but mainly because they love the very different sensations that each small area of their garden presents as they move around it. We were completely surprised by the contrast between the original cottage garden and the leading-edge twenty-first-century garden designs of Paul Cooper and Judy Toll. Full marks to the Allens for daring to be contemporary. ▼

A living willow dome (above) with a window and a living willow seat looks on to the meadow tended for twenty-five years.

The Allens (opposite) are using to the full their attractive and serene garden of meditation.

Waddesdon Manor

WADDESDON, BUCKINGHAMSHIRE

A variation on Victorian parterre planting (below) using marigolds within a narrow range of colours.

Formal parterres (opposite) were always part of grand Victorian gardens and this one has been completely restored by landscape designer Beth Rothschild.

Guy: I think it's fascinating to see how the ribbons of colour are used, how they meld one into the other and how different-coloured leaves create interest in the parterre. Gordon: I really like this, too. Call me an old-fashioned Yank, but I think the nineteenth-century parterre is a bit too blowsy. In fact I think some of the colours are an irritant on the retina.

Waddesdon Manor, an enormous house in the French style, was built by Lord Ferdinand Rothschild in 1874 on the windy summit of Lodge Hill. In order to create a site large enough for the house, the top of the hill had to be sliced off to an average depth of 3m

(10ft) over an area of 4 hectares (10 acres). A steam tramway was built to take the earth spoil away and to bring the building materials up to the site where the Château-de-Blois-inspired country pile was to be erected.

The main gardens were designed by a Frenchman and are comparatively formal. The reception rooms on the garden side overlook a wide terrace in which there have always been parterres filled with annual bedding plants. The landscape beyond falls away to great swathes of green meadow where groups of trees have been planted to frame and enhance the view.

The Victorian garden required tremendous upkeep. Beth Rothschild told us about a letter written by Lady Warwick when she was staying at Waddesdon. Apparently, she arrived at the house on a wet Friday evening and noticed that all the geraniums in the parterre had been flattened by the rain. Early the following morning she woke to the sound of an army of gardeners replanting the beds in a completely new pattern. It could take 300,000 plants to effect such a change, and the Rothschilds usually altered the parterres at least three times each summer. The designs always incorporated the family emblem of five red arrows bound together, representing the five sons of Nathan Rothschild, sent all over Europe to establish the family-run extensions of his banking empire.

Aided by a computer, installation of the parterre's carpet bedding (opposite) took ten hours instead of eight weeks.

Twenty-first-century interpretation of carpet bedding inspired by the changing light on the fountain pool.

on plants. In fact, I even stole a plant when I was seven. I was so terrified that my mother or father would find out that I hid this tiny little cactus in the bathroom cupboard. It died, of course. By the age of fourteen I had my own greenhouse ... I left school at sixteen, spent a year at horticultural college, another three years at Kew and I have been gardening ever since.'

Beth is now a garden designer and she is in charge of everything that happens in the gardens at Waddesdon. She has no wish to work in a garden which is a simple historic recreation: 'We want to recreate a true Victorian garden, but we also want to go forward, and move into the next millennium. We want to do new things, contemporary things, so that people are drawn to come back and see new ideas.'

The parterres on the main terrace are laid out with complex designs created with carpet bedding. A definition of this style, so popular with the Victorians, was given by Robert Johnson in his *Gardener's Assistant*, published in 1878: '... a system of bedding in which neat and dwarf growing foliage plants are used in the form of mosaic, geometrical or other designs'.

In 1999 Lord Rothschild and his daughter decided that two of the main parterre beds should be redesigned by John Hubbard, an American artist living in England who specialises in abstract landscape painting.

Waddesdon became the property of the National Trust in 1957 and the fifty-four gardeners of the late nineteenth century were reduced to ten. Much more recently, Lord Rothschild has become passionately interested in the preservation and restoration of Waddesdon. He was determined to bring the house and gardens back to the condition of their Victorian heyday.

Lord Rothschild's daughter Beth is an equally determined character. Since she was a child, all she has ever wanted to do is garden. In her own words, it made a touching story:

'I used to go and spend my pocket money

WE WANT TO RECREATE A TRUE VICTORIAN GARDEN,
BUT WE ALSO WANT TO GO FORWARD,
AND MOVE INTO THE NEXT MILLENNIUM.

The first design was installed in 1999. This trial run kept eight gardeners fully employed over five weeks, installing 50,000 plants. By the time it was finished, morale was low and everyone was bored.

Soon after this first trial had been completed, Richard and Chris Harnett of Kernock Park Plants in Cornwall appeared, bringing with them a wonderful high-tech system for installing bedding schemes. Their method is very popular with town councils, large corporations and other organisations that favour the use of complex floral displays. John Hubbard's new design, which was inspired by the movement of water and the reflections in the great Baroque fountain at the centre of the parterre, was scanned on to a computer and then translated into a grid. The computer produced a template for each square of the grid, which the Harnetts, appropriately enough, refer to as 'carpet tiles'. The exact number and colour of plants shown on each template was then planted in a tray filled with peat-free compost. When they arrived at Waddesdon, the trays were already marked with a code relating to their exact position in the design. They were then fitted together like an enormous jigsaw. The two carpet beds take a total of 900 boxes, containing 50,000 plants in all. It took only eight people to install them over a period of ten hours, thus reducing labour costs to an absolute minimum, while creating an immediate effect and instant satisfaction for all concerned.

It was amazing to watch the trays being installed with complete confidence and great skill, under the watchful eye of John Hubbard and Beth Rothschild. Work continued throughout the day, despite two rainstorms. By 5 o'clock, the weather had become golden and the carpet bedding, mainly in pale acid, jade and sage greens, greys, mauves, pale orange and a streak of red, looked quite miraculous in the late-afternoon sun, all abstract watery ribbons and diamonds. Attention to detail has always been the hallmark of the Rothschild family, and it seemed that their enthusiasm for any undertaking remains undiminished. ▼

Kerscott

SWIMBRIDGE, DEVON

Engraved on the slate disc
(right) in the centre of the
Duncan foot labyrinth is the
splendid line from T. S. Eliot's
Four Quartets, 'At the still point
of the turning world.'

A former slurry lagoon (opposite)
has been transformed into an
elegant circular reflecting pool.

Jessica Duncan: I've always been interested in plants, but primarily it's space and what to do with it that interests me. If you are living in a space you must really look around it, above it and below it, and do what you can to make it relate to where you are. Perhaps if the planners spent time, as we do in our gardens, it might help the planning processes in towns and cities.

Jessica and Peter Duncan moved to an old dairy farm near Swimbridge in 1984. The early years were spent clearing away concrete foundations, demolishing old cow cubicles and filling in drainage ditches. The circular slurry lagoon was eventually transformed into an elegant pond.

The landscape at the back of the house extends to 2.8 hectares (7 acres) and Jessica, who is a follower of the site-generated school of design, has allowed the rise and fall of the ground to inspire the design and planting of the garden. The first problem was the lack of a central focus on the garden side of the house. This meant that there was no point from which a satisfactory vista or central axis could be drawn from the house to the garden boundary. This difficulty has been overcome by the planting of a rather formal garden in which a mid-point has been established nearer to the house. This is a pool surrounded by a clipped *Lonicera nitida aurea* hedge from which a couple of topiary animal figures are now beginning to emerge. Paths run to either side of the pool, one leading to a barn studio and the other flanking an old wall covered with roses.

In order to give protection from the wind a mixture of trees and shrubs were planted fifteen years ago around the perimeter of the garden. The planting is not too dense, so it does not completely screen the 'borrowed' landscape beyond. There is also a stream connecting various pools and rills. These give the impression of being quite natural because they follow the contours of the landscape. This year the round pond made from the old slurry lagoon has been altered to give better reflections, and irregular swirls of golden gravel have been laid along the edges of it.

By walking the land in all seasons, Jessica has realised that the land-forms themselves

THE WHOLE GARDEN IS A TWENTY-FIRST-CENTURY VARIATION
ON 'THE GENIUS OF THE PLACE'.

have dictated the use to which the land could be put over the centuries. This realisation has always informed her decisions, about both the design and the planting of the garden. Much of her inspiration takes place in winter, when she sees the bones of the garden without what she calls 'its summer camouflage' of leaves on trees and shrubs. This is the moment for decisions about the shape and design of the site.

On a far side of the garden there is a cornus hedge in which Jessica has inserted a line of dogwood cuttings that she has trimmed to mirror the profile of a prominent hill about a mile away. The line is further enforced by an interweaving of willow twigs and the form of an overhanging branch of hawthorn.

The experience of going around Jessica's garden is one of amazing satisfaction and constant discovery. Nothing is ever wasted. When the barn adjoining the front garden blew down, its remains were transformed into a sheltered site for less hardy plants. Similarly, the grove below the pond is made up of saplings salvaged from another site. At its centre there is a foot labyrinth about 5.4m (18ft) in diameter. Paths made from stone setts and grass lead to a slate disc at the centre of the labyrinth. Engraved in the slate are T. S. Eliot's words from 'Burnt Norton' in the *Four Quartets*: 'At the still point of the turning world.'

This is one of the very few examples we have seen of a site-generated private garden. The landscape glimpsed through the dogwood and willow sculpture is not only a mirror for the shapes that Jessica has created, it is a source of inspiration that changes with the light and the seasons. The whole garden is a twenty-first-century variation on 'the genius of the place' which, with Jessica Duncan's enthusiasm and infallible eye, is becoming more beautiful and more remarkable with every passing year. ▼

Jessica Duncan (above) stands at the entry to her foot labyrinth.

The main design of the garden (opposite) is based on the natural change of levels and a glimpse through to the fields beyond.

A cornus hedge with a line of woven willow mimicking the curve of the distant hill, a wonderful example of site-generated design.

Corpusty

CORPUSTY, NORFOLK

Roger Last (below) has spent the last forty years creating on his Norfolk property incidents from the history of gardens from Roman times to the twenty-first century.

Fibreoptic lighting (opposite) dramatises and utilises this truly wonderful garden every night of the year.

Gordon: The *trompe l'oeil* coffering of the cupola is decaying most pleasingly.
Guy: And if I may say so Mr Taylor, it looks as though one of those gods may be about to fall on your head.
Gordon: You know Guy, you should just eradicate that hopeful note from your voice ...

Roger Last's garden covers about 2 hectares (5 acres). When they began to make a garden in the mid-sixties, the Lasts had no grand plan. The garden has gradually taken shape and, as Roger says himself, 'It is not a garden of rooms ... it's a garden of spaces that flow from one to another.' There

are a series of references to garden history but, in Roger's words: 'Nothing is copied. In my view, copies never work. The design is based on the style and spirit of different periods.'

The four-chambered grotto was built in the shadow of an enormous chestnut tree. Roger told us that they chose the site because 'the canopy of the leaves was so dense that very little light penetrated and it was so dry that nothing would grow. It was a dead space and it seemed the perfect site for a grotto.' It took over fifteen years to construct, using the local Carr building stone, found near Sandringham. The dense leaves of the chestnut mean that the building is almost completely dark inside during the summer. Roger is particularly satisfied by the effect of movement '... from dark areas into the light and back into pools of darkness again'. The entrance to the building is at an upper level. The dimly lit head of a classical river god can be glimpsed just before you descend to the lower level through a dark passage. Here, in a mysteriously lit niche, is a bronze snake dripping water. Overhead clerestories let in the lowest possible level of light, making visitors feel spooked and vulnerable like initiates at Samothrace or Eleusis.

In another area a two-storey tower has been built to imitate a Gothic ruin. From the top there are views of many parts of the garden, although the superior design of the

site ensures that nothing is entirely exposed. A narrow path from the tower takes you through another dark corridor into a domed room with, as Roger says, '... every possible reference to the Classical past'. The coffering on the ceiling is a convincing *trompe l'oeil* painting which is beginning to show beautiful signs of decay and there are roundels containing the heads of Roman emperors. From the outside it looks like a Palladian villa, perhaps the Villa Rotunda, cut down to the scale of a classy garden shed. Pedimented wings have been added to the outside, making two of the prettiest Classical compost containers imaginable. The result could almost be Pompeii come to Norfolk.

Roger put new windows into his sitting room last year and cut down the trees that grew immediately beyond them. Once he had created the space, he decided that he must make a new garden to fill it. His first impulse was to create a Jacobean knot garden, but he rejected that and decided to go for something contemporary. In the end he came to the following conclusion: 'I decided that the design should be relatively simple, but strongly geometric. It should have form to the fore and no flowers at all.' The new design is indeed geometric. For Roger it proved to be 'the most challenging of all the garden designs I have installed'. The chief challenge lay in using new materials: '... a traditional garden has brick and stone

and both of them age very well. They get this patina of decay on them which we all love. In a modern garden you have stainless steel, acrylic and crushed glass. We don't want that to weather, do we, we don't want a pattern of ageing. It has to look crisp and new.'

The wall at the third and uppermost level of the garden has two square stainless-steel panels set into it. Elsewhere, pairs of pyramids made from stainless steel and acrylic in diminishing sizes give a wonderful sense of perspective. The stepping stones across the pool are in York stone and white glass is used as a dressing. The planting consists of two long, raised box hedges on either side, which will eventually be cut to slope into the garden. Although the garden is contemporary in every way, Roger could not resist making links with the past here, just as he has elsewhere. It is for this reason that he has chosen to plant box, yew and pleached hornbeam, all of them timeless features in the garden. However, he uses the plants in a completely contemporary way to create a variety of geometric shapes. There are two blocks of the grey curry plant, *Helichrysum italicum*, which Roger patrols ruthlessly with secateurs, keeping it flowerless and perfectly minimal. Another two blocks are planted in the dark brown-red grass *Uncinia rubra*. Roger also manipulates light in the garden. In his own words: 'Natural light is reflected in the water, either lying still in the pool, or sparkling and moving in the water course and water column. Light is reflected in the stainless steel, bringing its own world of reflected sky, colour, cloud and sun, ever changing as the time, days and seasons revolve.'

At night a line of fibreoptic lights illuminates the water as it slips exquisitely down a stainless-steel column, through a central canal and then falls into the rectangular pool at the front of the design. By using electric light Roger has created a twenty-four-hour garden. As he says, he wanted to be able to appreciate the garden at 4 o'clock on a winter's evening, just as he would on a summer afternoon. Putting all the different elements of the new garden together proved quite complex but, as Roger says, 'We don't have problems in the twenty-first century, it's all challenges!'

A door on the far side of the main garden opens to the public path and another door opens into a miniature park with a lake. You are suddenly dropped into the eighteenth century. The trees have been planted to allow vistas through to the lake, which is fed by a lovely stretch of the River Bure. Occasional Classical busts are scattered about the landscape, and half a statue is waving, or possibly drowning, in the water of the lake. Some seats, sited apparently at random, create an effect of space and tranquillity. It comes as a great surprise to realise that you

are in the middle of a village and that real life goes on just beyond the driveway.

Two millennia of landscape design and architecture have inspired this garden. Nothing could be more dramatic than Roger Last's brilliant twenty-first-century minimalist design, which gives a really fitting welcome to the third millennium. ▼

A long, curved wall of Norfolk flint built in memory of Roger's brother, with whom he created the gardens.

Old Vicarage

EAST RUSTON, NORFOLK

Determination and resources can transform twelve acres (above) into a fine twentieth-century homage to seventeenth-century formal garden design.

The main vista (opposite), which could be from a grand seventeenth-century château, leads from the house to a series of enclosures to a dining pavilion 200 yards away.

Guy: Alan, we know that you get about 15,000 visitors a year through here ... What is the reaction to this part of the garden?
Alan: Oh, it's run the gamut from A to Z: incredulity, admiration and complete 'what the hell are they doing?' We have every kind of reaction you can possibly imagine, but I think the main one is of pure wonder.

Graham Robeson and Alan Gray bought the Old Vicarage at East Ruston in the early 1970s. They did not live there full time until 1986 and only commenced work on the garden in 1988. Their first task was to plant a wind-break all around the boundary. Many of the trees have now grown to a considerable size, causing some distress to the neighbours, who are sorry to lose the view of the church and vicarage which the trees now screen. Nevertheless, the wind-break has created a wonderful microclimate. The temperature hardly ever dips below freezing and, in this dry part of Norfolk, only about 25cm (10in) of rain falls each year.

For ten years or more Robeson and Gray dedicated their time to laying out a vast formal garden based on seventeenth-century French principles of design. A framework of tall, wide, yew-framed *allées* leads away from the house. The principal one leads from the south lawn, across the Green Court, into the King's Walk and finally to the pavilion and the Mediterranean Garden. To the left of the house are the Dutch Garden, the Sunken Garden, the Autumn Borders, the Acacia Avenue, the Spring Borders and the Holm Oak Walk. To the right is the Tropical Garden and the Walled Garden.

To our minds, the Desert Wash is the most interesting and spectacular feature in the garden. Robeson and Gray told us that they had been inspired to make it following a journey to the desert landscapes in the borderlands between California and Arizona. They have recreated both the arid landscape and the rough, rugged channels that are carved into it by the flood water that rips through the surface of the desert twice a year. They have also built a dry river bed. This is lined with water-worn pebbles of various sizes, creating the impression that water has been flowing along the river for millennia. A wooden bridge spans the river bed, adding to the illusion. This is an amazing semicircular construction designed by Robeson. Once the concrete foundations on either side had been made, it was constructed out of arcs and giant pegs of wood hammered and held together entirely by pressure. No nails, screws or glue have been used at all. Beneath the bridge is a little pool of water, designed to give the impression that it is about to dry up. This is in fact another illusion, as it is connected to a pipe and a recirculating pump.

The surface of the desert has been made up

ROBESON AND GRAY HAVE CREATED SOMETHING THAT WORKS
BOTH AS A HYMN TO DROUGHT-RESISTANT PLANTS AND
ALSO AS A TRULY CONTEMPORARY GARDEN FOR
THE TWENTY-FIRST CENTURY.

from the local stone, 163 tonnes (160 tons) of Norfolk flints, variously graded from 60cm (24in) in diameter down to fine pea gravel for the paths along the *arroyo*. The planting in this area of the garden is drawn from South Africa, Australia and Arizona. There are echiums, *Yucca gloriosa* and agapanthus, cistus, *Ceanothus* 'Ken Taylor', delosperma, agave, and some South African thistles that are allowed to seed and grow where they will. The rocky landscape, or, to use the current buzz word for it in American landscape architecture jargon, 'xeriscape', is monochrome in its dryness.

Robeson and Gray are beginning to find places in the Desert Wash for contemporary sculpture. The first piece they have bought was made from stone and rusty metal by a final-year student at Norwich School of Art. Gray has good strong views on contemporary sculpture in gardens: 'I don't think there is enough modern statuary in gardens. People always play safe and buy an Adonis, a Shepherd Boy, or a Cupid, or something. It's time some of these younger artists had the chance to show their work, not just younger artists either, but contemporary artists.'

Between the Desert Wash and the parish church is a 0.6 hectare (1.5 acre) meadow which, in mid-July, was a fabulous tapestry of poppies, cornflowers and daisies. The meadow was started by Robeson and Gray about six years ago and is maintained on the basic principle of seed being sown in the autumn, growth encouraged with a little fertiliser in the spring, and then the area left to its own devices until the flowers have bloomed, set seed and died back. It is mown in September. The stalks are left to dry, the seeds shaken from them and the stalk detritus is removed, then everything is fallow until the next year. Gray said that the meadow had never looked so beautiful as it did on the day we were, quite surreally, visiting a south-western USA desert wash in Norfolk. Robeson and Gray have created something that works both as a hymn to drought-resistant plants and also as a truly contemporary garden for the twenty-first century.

The Desert Wash (opposite) echoes the landscape of Arizona in Norfolk.

A broad selection of desert-loving plants (below) which thrive in Norfolk's limited rainfall, a mere ten inches per year.

Kiftsgate Court

CHIPPING CAMPDEN, GLOUCESTERSHIRE

A wonderfully serene twentieth-century design (above) of stone, water and grass enclosed by mature nineteenth-century yew hedges.

Water falls gently from each of the twenty-four gilded bronze philodendron leaves (opposite) and reflects beautifully in the black pool.

Guy: Funny, isn't it. We go round all these huge gardens belonging to other people and nobody guesses the size of our own garden.
Gordon: Our two little window boxes in Knightsbridge?
Guy: Exactly.
Gordon: Well, we're not the only ones. People might find it shocking but Sir Geoffrey Jellicoe, who loved designing gardens, didn't garden.

Kiftsgate Court's real claim to fame is the rose of the same name: *Rosa filipes* 'Kiftsgate', the largest rose in England. When the Kiftsgate rose at Kiftsgate Court was last measured, it was found to be 24m (80ft) x 27m (90ft) x 15m (50ft). Other specimens have been known to destroy the most innocent of garages and garden sheds. The rose is allowed to grow on various sites in the garden to its full, monstrous, majestic extent, and to see it in bloom with its multi-headed panicles of white flowers is a truly wondrous sight.

Kiftsgate is the quintessential English garden, a sort of Arts and Crafts Valhalla, loved and tended by a family who have been there for four generations. Within this traditional structure Mr and Mrs John Chambers have succeeded in creating a magical contemporary garden. Known as The Tennis Court Garden, their design really succeeds in delivering the shock of the new. In search of inspiration, they looked at as many photos as possible of modern and contemporary gardens. They were chiefly inspired by Sir Geoffrey Jellicoe's masterpiece at Sutton Place in Surrey. It was Jellicoe's formal canal and paving stones that really caught their imaginations. The design at Kiftsgate, like that of Sutton Place, is a play on space, scale and geometry, how rectangles can balance and interrelate and how they can enhance each other when some are grass, some are paved and others are filled with water.

The Tennis Court Garden lies within a rectangular yew enclosure. The Chamberses have created two large rectangles, a wide

grass area and a band around the edge of the space. Set within it is a large black reflecting pool, so engineered that the water appears to be on the same level as the grass surround. Within the water is a rectangle of turf. Access to the turf area in the middle of the pool is provided by rectangular paving stones. At one end of the pool, beyond the grassed area, there are twenty-four thin, black-painted, stainless-steel staves, each bearing a bronze cast of a philodendron leaf that has been nickel-plated and finally gold-washed. A recirculating pump, throttled right down, is used to make water fall with infinite gentleness into the pool below. Eventually the Chamberses hope the action of the water will wash away the gold leaf and the nickel so that only the gold veins will subtly bedizen the bronze leaves. What splendid contemporary magic in a traditional context!

After the rivalry of shapes and colours in the main part of the gardens, to enter this serene, minimalist sanctuary of contemporary garden design is to be immediately aware of a visual and mental peace. Here one begins to understand why, even in the most traditional gardens, there is room for a space which is a perfect reflection of contemporary style. This is a garden that displays the wonderful innovation taking place in garden design in Great Britain. ▼

The *demi-lune* swimming pool (opposite) set dramatically below the main garden terraces at Kiftsgate Court.

Scypen Garden

RINGMORE, DEVON

The Fibonacci Sequence and the spiral form were the inspirations for the design for the interconnecting pools (right).

An eccentric use of wine bottles, the Bottle House (opposite), a wonderful surreal surprise at the end of this garden.

Guy: I like the sempervivum here. If you crouched down very low, it would look just like a jungle.

Ann Bracey: Yes, if you were a mouse, or even smaller …

Gordon: Is that the English sense of whimsy?

Guy: Not at all. I look at that and see a jungle. If you tried, all you would see is a small plant.

The Braceys bought an old cowshed on approximately 0.4 hectare (1 acre) of land in Ringmore in 1980. It was an awkward site close to the Devon coast. Salt-laden gales off the sea, which is only about 0.8 km (0.5 miles) away, occasionally lash the garden at speeds of up to 112kph (70mph). John Bracey is an architect and the cowshed has developed into quite a large contemporary house for his family. It is called Scypen because that is the Old English word for a cowshed.

The garden is a very intricate interplay between the architect, who conceived the overall plan and the architectural elements within the garden, and the plantsmanship of his wife, Ann. Almost the first thing that you see on entering is a sundial made from the grooved bricks of the cowshed's original floor. The compass points are marked with blue bricks and the numbers are taken from a very old clock golf set. The gnomon was made from a rod given to Bracey when he was a child – waste not want not! The sundial is set slightly differently from Greenwich Mean Time as there is a difference of approximately eight seconds between midday at Greenwich and midday in this part of Devon.

To the left of the sundial is the Fibonacci Wall. Its design is based on the twelfth-century Fibonacci Sequence invented by Leonardo Fibonacci, the first outstanding mathematician of the Middle Ages. In the Fibonacci Sequence each number is equal to the sum of the preceding two (1, 1, 2, 3, 5, 8 …). The numbers have spiral applications in astronomy, zoology and botany. The seed and petal structures of many plants, including the dahlia and the sunflower, are often double spirals following a defined set of numbers. Bracey's Fibonacci Wall is capped at its curved climax with an unusual rotating stone globe of the world, mounted to celebrate the coming of the third millennium.

Beyond the sundial is the Fountain of Life, a series of pools with a design based on DNA spirals. The three interlocking pools are

edged with flints laid in a spiral pattern. The design is entirely contemporary, and yet the reverse spirals also recall the running pattern used by the ancient Greeks and derived from ocean waves.

The Silver Garden beside the pool is surprisingly traditional in the context of this fascinating site. It was made to commemorate the Braceys' twenty-fifth wedding anniversary. The silver theme is conveyed by a planting of *Helichrysum petiolaris*, *Stachys byzantina* 'Silver Carpet' and *Artemisia alba canescens*.

The garden is always changing. Garden surprises abound and in the trail that leads the grandchildren and their friends from the house to the furthest corner of the site, they will now find an immense bottle-shaped structure made, naturally, from bottles. Bracey has used recycled green wine bottles from the local pub as his building material. The lower courses of the edifice are made from 1.5 litre bottles and 1 litre bottles are used for the rest, resulting in a truly architectural set of proportions. The bottle tops face inwards, creating an amazing, enclosed space in which the children can play. The inside of the house is illuminated by a strange green light. It forms an eccentric climax to this fascinating garden which is a compromise between the vision and discipline of an architect and the knowledge and enthusiasm of a plantswoman. ▼

A home-made sundial (opposite) set on Ringmore, Devon, time rather than the more usual Greenwich Mean Time.

Little Sparta

DUNSYRE, LANARKSHIRE, SCOTLAND

Ian Hamilton Finlay (above), poet and garden maker, is always considering how to change and improve his masterly garden.

A pair of stone hand grenades as finials (opposite) are Finlay's idiosyncratic reworking of the traditional pineapples.

Ian Hamilton Finlay, a fine poet and a great garden maker, has been driven by culture, not just by horticulture. He moved to this small cottage surrounded by 2 hectares (5 acres) of land on a barren hillside in Lanarkshire about thirty years ago. The house was originally called Stonypath because the name accurately described the route to it across the fields. When Finlay had a huge row with Strathclyde Council over the rates, he changed the name to Little Sparta. That battle dragged on for quite a long time, just like the war between Athens and Sparta in 431–404 BC. Sparta finally won, as did Finlay.

In Sir Roy Strong's opinion, Little Sparta is 'the only really original garden made in this country in the last fifty years'. Classical sources and myths are an integral part of the garden landscape. There are frequent references to Finlay's obsessions: mythology, the French Revolution, the sea and boats. Pieces of sculpture with beautiful inscriptions engraved on them or other elements such as broken columns or half-hidden pediments remind you of other places and other times.

Little Sparta is reminiscent both of Imperial Katsura in Kyoto, Japan, and of England's Stourhead in Wiltshire. Just as at Little Sparta, these sites are best appreciated by following the specified path through the landscape. In each case, there is a masterful use of space.

The first area at Little Sparta consists of two 'sacred' groves. Gaps in the hedgerow allow carefully orchestrated glimpses over the Pentland Hills. A long concrete path leading to one of the entrances of the house is inscribed with a list of names to describe different kinds of boat: yawl, buccaneer, barge, quinquireme, lugger, dhurry, sloop, brigantine, brig, schooner, ship, ketch and wherry. There is a group of birch trees and on one is a stone plaque inscribed with the words 'Bring Back the Birch'; Finlay's wonderful wit is ever present in the gardens of Little Sparta.

Bridge of two wooden planks (left) with one of many mottoes at Little Sparta, 'That which joins and that which divides is one and the same.'

Overlooking the lochan, or small Scottish lake (opposite), is a thought by Saint–Just, 'The Present Order is the Disorder of the Future'.

Paths lead beyond the modest house to a large open area with a pool, in the middle of which there is a pillar with a warship. The Garden Temple (*casus belli* of the 'Little Spartan' Wars) stands nearby. It has painted stucco Corinthian-style pilasters. And on another side of the pool is a store house with columns to either side of its door dedicated to Baucis and Philemon, the demi-gods of hospitality. By the pool is an exquisite stone scallop shell inscribed 'Caddis Shell, Goddess Shell'. References to Venus and shells are myriad throughout the garden.

The ominous grey slate sculpture, *Nuclear Sail*, emerges (above) between a bank of bulrushes and clouds of rosebay willow herb.

In a grove of birch (opposite) there is another of Finlay's witty tags, 'Bring Back the Birch'.

Always unique and memorable for us will be this exquisite shell, the delicate carving and the extremely faint but insistent trickle of water when we heard it first on a still, hot summer's day.

Beyond this area where Finlay lives, works and designs is another woodland area with a path punctuated with many other stone, wooden and bronze carved plaques and sculptures. The path meanders towards a perfect miniature of a Roman aqueduct. Nearby, the gigantic gilded head of Apollo stands, with 'Apollon Terroriste' engraved on his forehead, a dual homage to Classical mythology and the French Revolution.

Close to Lochan Eck ('lochan' being Scots for a small loch or lake), are eleven pieces of stone engraved with the words 'The Present Order is the Disorder of the Future', a provocative insight from the late-eighteenth-century philosopher, Saint-Just. Nearby, on the edge of the lake, is a sculpture in black slate entitled *Nuclear Sail*. Beside it in the water is a small wooden boat with a fabulous terracotta-coloured sail.

Recently Finlay has created a water meadow. This new design demonstrates his continuing mastery of water, stone, grass, plant material, trees and, most importantly, space. He is now of a venerable age and is no longer active in the construction and maintenance of the garden. He is always planning new elements, however, and different surprises, ensuring that the garden landscape is always changing and improving. His enduring concern is with the ideas that a garden generates and the definition of the ideal landscape. Finlay loves the philosophy and the art of the ancient Greeks, the Romans, the Italian Renaissance and the French Revolution, but he says that he has little time for contemporary art. To his mind, Tate Modern is a wonderful building, pity about the contents!

Even in the pouring rain Finlay's garden at Little Sparta is rich with amazing layers of meaning and a wonderful sense of aesthetic well-being. ▼

Belsay Hall

THE SITOOTERIES OF BELSAY HALL, PONTELAND, NORTHUMBERLAND

You Make Me Feel Mighty Real (right) is this jolly bespangled miniature church.

In the quarry garden (opposite) is a white cube broken open which becomes the *Rocky Love Seat.*

A folly ... might be defined as a useless building erected for ornament on a gentlemen's estate, but that would apply equally well to garden temples, and there is a world of difference between temples and follies. Certainly, temples are generally in a classical style, and follies in a Gothic, but that is only part of the truth. There is also a difference of mood; a temple is an ornament, a folly is glass, and bones and hanks of weeds. Follies are built for pleasure, and pleasure is personal, and difficult to define. Follies are fashionable or frantic, built to keep up with the neighbours, or built from obsession. They are at once cheerful or morbid, both an ornament for a gentleman's grounds and a mirror for his mind.

Barbara Jones, *Follies and Grottoes,* 1953

There has been a castle at Belsay for more than 600 years, and in the early nineteenth century, the finest Neo-Classical, honey-coloured stone mansion was built at a short distance from the original site. The path from the castle to the hall passes through the quarries which supplied the stone for the building of both; they are both conserved in a state of disrepair, roofed but entirely empty; twenty-first-century deconstruction curatorship comes to English Heritage?

The 12 hectares (30 acres) of grounds and landscape, including woodlands, wild gardens and ruins connecting the buildings, transmute from great formality in front of Belsay Hall, to winding paths through the abandoned quarries. Here the stone cliffs tower above the paths. The planting appears to be naturalistic, but it is carefully chosen for the shady situation and designed to look as decorative as possible throughout the year. It is here, inside and outside, that the sitooteries have been placed. This is the praiseworthy and unique exhibition of contemporary pavilions and summerhouses commissioned by English Heritage as part of its Year of Public Sculpture 2000.

A sitooterie is the Scots word for an outside shelter, a place to 'sit out in', to read, to look at the landscape, to have a meal or even arrange an amorous tryst. In garden history terms they are usually known as follies, and they might be inspired by

gazebos, temples, pagodas, grottoes or pavilions. Another witty definition of a folly comes from leading folly fanatic Gwyn Headley: 'An over-ambitious and useless structure, preferably with a wildly improbable local legend attached. But in real life … follies defy even such broad definitions. The folly must lie in the eye of the beholder.'

Eleven sitooteries were built at Belsay for the exhibition. Inside the Hall there was *Dumb Waiter* by Simon Watkinson, where two window blinds, one made of white china, and the other of knives and forks, were rigged so that they moved up and down over three storeys of windows, one above the other, some 10.5m (35ft) in height. Perhaps symbols of the endless downstairs drudgery have been elevated to the upstairs.

The Hairy Sitooterie is on the edge of the first terrace and, sideways on, looks like an immense stationary porcupine. It is in fact a square metal box covered with 5,200 wooden staves. It has a bridge leading to the front opening, where a gap on the opposite side frames a view of the landscape.

Rest Area by Julian Opie is built on the path towards the quarries. It consists of nine rectangles made of steel and black glass with an orange-coloured roof like a garage. When you enter, you find yourself in a maze where you are left to twist and turn from one side to the other, until you come out eventually in the woods beyond the quarry.

A little further along is *You Make Me Feel Mighty Real* by FAT, which is in a spectacular church-like form covered in dark blue, pale blue and silver spangles. The interior is bright pink, with a skylight and a window looking into the landscape beyond.

Finally, in the quarry is *Rocky Love Seat* by Tania Kovats, made apparently of a white square of stone, broken in half to reveal natural rock formations inside, cunningly arranged to create a seating area. It is, in fact, a steel cube with a fibreglass interior. All the sitooteries are extraordinary, and follies in the true sense, to make the viewer marvel.

The sitooteries exhibition was the brainchild of the Belsay curator, Judith King. Both she and English Heritage should be given the highest praise for provocatively showing that the contemporary British garden summerhouse is both incredibly alive and most imaginatively well in the twenty-first century. What a pity that it was only a temporary exhibition. ▼

A spiny cabin (opposite) dares you to enter and have a rest in *The Hairy Sitooterie.*

Enclosed Plane (left) is where a rectangle of aluminium and canvas opens up to become a seat or sitooterie with a protective canopy.

Earth Labyrinth

GALLOWAY FOREST, DUMFRIESSHIRE, SCOTLAND

A silken thread could lead you through the Galloway Forest to this earthen labyrinth

Deep in the spruce and pine woods of the Galloway Forest in south-west Scotland is a magical, quiet clearing which is probably visited more by red deer than 'culture vulture' human beings. In it is what might appear to be a very large archaeological relic from the Bronze Age. Only the informed will recognise the raised earth labyrinth as the work of Jim Buchanan, one of Britain's foremost Land Artists.

Constructed in 1999, the labyrinth is built up to about 1 m (3 ft) above ground level. The paths have a pale top dressing of stone chippings. Darker pebbles have been laid between them and the slopes have been seeded with wild local grasses. At the centre of the labyrinth there is a cairn. Jim hopes that visitors will add a stone from the landscape of their own home to it, and contributions from Belgium and the Netherlands are already in evidence. The water that wells out from the centre of the cairn is a symbol of renewal. The system is gravity-fed from a stream on the hillside above.

Buchanan's work on labyrinths reflects a more general renewal of interest in forming and sculpting the land, using the very stuff of the earth, its soil, as the medium of artistic expression. His first Land Art commission was the Earth and Wildflower Labyrinth, built in 1996 at Tapton Park, Chesterfield. It is 130m (416ft) in diameter, with earth berms 1.2m (3.8ft) high. Buchanan's crew shifted 7,100 tonnes (7,000 tons) of soil during the construction of the labyrinth, which is the largest in Britain. It takes about 20 minutes to complete the 2.4 km (1.5 mile) circuit.

The labyrinth is among the most ancient shapes known to humankind. The maze is its synonym. Buchanan is clear about the difference between the two forms: 'A maze gives you options at every turn. A labyrinth leads you around a course to the centre.' All major cultures have used the labyrinth at some point in their history.

YOU CAN TAKE LABYRINTHS SERIOUSLY AS A FORM OF
MEDITATION AND PILGRIMAGE,
OR YOU CAN JUST ENJOY THEM
AS PUBLIC ART AND SOMEWHERE FOR A WALK.
Jim Buchanan

Madresfield Court

A large yew maze (right) in which the BBC encouraged us to lose our way!

Lady Morrison, chatelaine of Madresfield Court (opposite), walking her dogs through an avenue of cedars planted 150 years ago.

Guy: Fascinating, a lime arcade.
Gordon: It's an arbour.
Guy: What's the difference?
Gordon: Well, an arcade is more architectural. Stones and cement, Rue de Rivoli, you know. This is an arbour.
Guy: OK, you call it an arbour, but I'll go on calling it an arcade.

Lady Morrison's family have lived at Madresfield Court for at least 800 years. There can be very few people in Great Britain capable of tracing their genealogy with such certainty to the same place for a comparable length of time. Lady Morrison is always aware of the generations of forebears who created the landscape in which she lives.

Madresfield is a very large, archetypal English country house, begun by the Normans and completed during the Victorian era. It stands at the centre of a large estate and has gardens extending to 24 hectares (60 acres). It is said that the house and the Lygon-Beauchamp family who lived in it were the inspiration for Evelyn Waugh's *Brideshead Revisited*, written in 1944. Being in private hands, it is almost entirely unknown to the world at large.

The original garden of Madresfield Court was lost when the house was altered and enlarged between 1860 and 1889. Lady Morrison's grandfather employed a staff of sixty to care for the gardens. Now there are only three gardeners and as a result many of the nineteenth-century gardens named after members of the family, such as Lady Mary's Garden and Lady Susan's Garden, have gone, as have the 1.6 hectares (4 acres) of walled kitchen garden. The semicircular perennial border may also be on its way out, releasing a full-time gardener for other, more necessary tasks. The border connects with a pretty semicircular arbour of pollarded limes, underplanted with masses of spring-flowering bulbs. The pollarded trees are reminiscent of the pretty lines of trees that you see in the main squares of French towns.

Madresfield Court has always had a moat because it was once a castle. The main reception rooms look across a wide paved terrace area to the moat. The terrace used to be planted with labour-intensive annuals in high Victorian style. Lady Morrison has wisely had the rectangular beds planted with single species of perennial herbs. Lavender, helichrysum and thyme make a simple,

minimalist twenty-first-century carpet, drawing the eye across the moat to the yew hedges, the fields and the further reaches of the estate. The varied greens of the herbs, the moat reflecting the sky and the formal rose beds create the foreground of the wonderful view.

Framing this view are venerable and beautifully clipped yew hedges and a Neo-Baroque fountain focal point. Yew buttresses once enclosed a series of complicated and highly labour-intensive Victorian flower-beds. Lady Morrison's reasons for removing these were as much aesthetic as economic.

Three avenues, each almost 0.5 km (0.25 miles) long, form triangles in the garden area. One of them is planted with Atlantic cedar, the second with *Quercus cerris* and *Quercus borealis*, two types of oak. The third is of Lombard poplars. Of course, the poplars grow faster than anything else, and consequently die faster, too. Since Lady Morrison took over the gardens seven years ago she has begun a systematic programme of felling old and diseased poplar trees. Cuttings from the original avenue have been planted in the gaps. This is a real project for the future, and Lady Morrison admits that she hopes the new avenue will be enjoyed by her grandchildren.

We usually hate rockeries, especially those twiddly little Victorian and Edwardian ones. Even rockery haters like us had to admire the

Pulhamite rocks installed at Madresfield in 1878. Pulhamite, invented by Mr Pulham, was an artificial rock, the nineteenth-century version of the fibreglass rocks that people make now. All the rocks look as though they come from an ancient quarry face, but it's pure fakery. Underneath the coloured concrete surface is a core of rubble. The Madresfield rockery is probably one of the best surviving examples of its kind in the country. Nature has been allowed to take over and the result is enchanting. A mass of grasses and ferns grow in the artificial crevices of the rocks, along with a variety of wild flowers.

A sense of great tranquillity pervades the gardens of Madresfield and the landscape beyond, suggesting that they have always led an untroubled existence. How long this will go on we cannot tell, but the present incumbent is doing her best to ensure that anyone lucky enough to be invited to Madresfield Court in 100 years' time will be awed by its beauty and peacefulness. ▼

A view from some of the main rooms across the parterre (opposite) recently planted with twentieth-century minimalist blocks of herbs for easier maintenance.

A display of nineteenth-century garden geometry (left), beautifully manicured yew hedges with buttresses framing a formal fountain.

Elsing Hall

EAST DEREHAM, NORFOLK

Shirley and David Cargill (right) leaning against a nineteenth-century cupola marking the entrance of their sixteenth-century house.

Secret garden (opposite) where the tip of a nineteenth-century church spire is the focal point of a twenty-first-century minimalist garden.

Shirley Cargill: These colours all go together beautifully, and they don't detract from each other.
Gordon: They don't clash. I know it's an old cliché, but there is still that British thing of putting red salvias with marigolds.
Shirley Cargill: I think it's called perverse.
Gordon: I think it's called municipal.

Elsing Hall was built in the fifteenth century and refaced and partly refenestrated in the nineteenth. As a result, it gives the impression of being a Victorian copy of a fifteenth-century manor house rather than the genuine article. The Cargills bought the house more than forty years ago and have had to test their knowledge and resources to restore it and to lay out a garden which gives the impression of great longevity. They call their style of gardening 'informal formality', an approach which sometimes gets them into trouble with their visitors. 'We really upset some people,' Shirley told us. It's largely a question of tidiness. A prime offence is their refusal to cut back perennial plants in autumn – they would hate to miss out on the wonderful effects of hoar frost on seed heads.

On the garden side of the house there are three wide terraces that lead down from the house to the moat. From a distance, the plants on the three terraces appear to rise to a third of the height of the house. Evergreen phlomis grows among escallonia and geraniums. In between are great stands of old-fashioned roses, with wonderful names like 'Archduc Joseph', 'Zigeunerknabe' and 'Frühlingsmorgen'. These were fading, so there was a wonderful billowing effect created by the pink and white roses, the white of the phlomis and the escallonia, combined with bands of rampant fennel, hollyhocks and delphiniums growing between the house and the moat.

The moat is fed by four natural springs. Blanket weed, caused by the nitrogen farmers

put on the land nearby, is a problem in the shallower water. 'It's going to be a Mississippi swamp,' David told us. 'I'm going to get crocodiles and small children ...' In the deeper areas the water is crystalline, reflecting some willows to one side and an arboretum on the other. There is also a meadow scattered with poppies.

There is only one bridge spanning the moat, so in order to explore the rest of the garden it is necessary to walk through the arboretum and to cross two streams, pass the winter beds and go finally to an arch which leads to an arbour of limes. This arbour is the first moment of formality in the garden. It leads you to a wall pierced by a gate. Through it you can just see a vertical focal point. This is made from the top of a church spire rescued from a reclamation yard. It sits in the middle of a formally planted grid of sixty-four clipped yews, inspired vaguely by the church spire and under-planted with lavender and cat mint. The whole area represents a game played with scale, shape and form and, as David says, 'It rests the eye.' It is the Cargills' twenty-first-century minimalist salute to contemporary garden design, even though it was planted in 1992. Although the design is quite large, it could be scaled down to create the perfect layout for the back garden of a town house.

In the spring this wonderful minimalist garden is outlined with long ribbons of white tulips. As it is enclosed by a wall, one comes across the garden completely unexpectedly, and leaves it just as suddenly by going through another gate.

The garden of Elsing Hall is an extraordinary creation. In many ways it is a timeless, dreamy English garden, but it is also very contemporary. Along with the minimalist garden, there are also modern sculptures scattered through the garden. David Cargill is a director of the Angela Flowers Gallery, dealing in contemporary art in London and Los Angeles.

The Cargills are always changing the garden so that each visit to Elsing will create a different impression. Whatever the season, it will always be an enchanting pilgrimage to the gardens of Elsing Hall. In winter huge drifts of snowdrops, aconites and species daffodils dominate, followed by masses and masses of hellebores in early spring and a splendid collection of climber, rambler and old roses in summer. The billowing, romantic perennial border left, more or less, to look after itself, is the highlight of late autumn. David told us that people often say, 'I see you are cutting down on staff' when they visit the garden. 'Actually,' he says, 'the staff are the two of us, and we're working like mad!' ▼

Select Bibliography

AND SUGGESTED FURTHER READING

GARDENS TRADITIONAL

Amherst, The Hon. Alicia. *A History of Gardening in England.* Quaritch, London 1895

Bean, W.J. *Trees and Shrubs Hardy in the British Isles* (4 vols). John Murray, London 1970

Bisgrove, Richard. *The National Trust Book of the English Garden.* Viking, London 1990

Brookes, John. All of his books on design and plants

Coats, Peter. *Great Gardens of Britain.* Artus, London 1977

Cooper, Guy and Gordon Taylor. *English Herb Gardens.* Weidenfeld and Nicolson, London 1985

Cooper, Guy and Gordon Taylor. *English Water Gardens.* Weidenfeld and Nicolson, London 1986

Crowe, Sylvia. *Garden Design.* Country Life, London 1965

Gothein, Marie Luise. *A History of Garden Art.* (2 vols). J.M. Dent and Sons, London 1928

Hadfield, Miles, Robert Harling and Leonie Highton. *British Gardeners: A Biographical Dictionary.* Zwemmer and Condé Nast, London 1980

Hay, Roy and Kenneth A. Beckett. *Reader's Digest Encyclopaedia of Garden Plants and Flowers.* London 1971

Headley, Gwyn and Wim Meulenkamp. *Follies: a National Trust Guide.* Jonathan Cape, London 1986

Hobhouse, Penelope. *Private Gardens of England.* Weidenfeld and Nicolson, London 1986

Hunt, John Dixon. *The Genius of the Place.* Elek, London 1975

Huxley, Anthony. *An Illustrated History of Gardening.* London 1978

Huxley, Anthony and Mark Griffiths. *The New Royal Horticultural Society Dictionary of Gardening* (4 vols). Macmillan, London 1992

Hyams, Edward. *Capability Brown and Humphry Repton.* Scribners, New York 1970

Jekyll, Gertrude. All of her books on plants and traditional design

Jellicoe, Geoffrey and Susan, Patrick Goode and Michael Lancaster. *The Oxford Companion to Gardens.* Oxford University Press, Oxford and New York 1986

Jellicoe, Geoffrey and Susan. *The Landscape of Man.* Thames and Hudson, London 1987

Strong, Roy and Julia Trevelyan Oman. *A Celebration of Gardens.* Harper Collins, London 1991

Tipping, H. Avray. *English Gardens.* Country Life, London 1925

GARDENS ECCENTRIC

Beardsley, John. *Gardens of Revelation.* Abbeville Publishing, New York 1995

Clarke, Ethne and George Wright. *English Topiary Gardens.* Weidenfeld and Nicolson, London 1988

Coleby, Nicola (ed.). *A Surreal Life: Edward James.* The Royal Pavilion, Libraries and Museums, Brighton and Hove, in association with Philip Watson Publishers, London 1998

Cooper, Guy and Gordon Taylor. *Gardens of Obsession: Eccentric and Extravagant Visions.* Weidenfeld and Nicolson, London 1999

Cornwall, Martin. *The Complete Book of the Gnome: All You'll Ever Need or Want to Know.* AA Publishing, Basingstoke, Hampshire 1997

Elliott, Brent, Dr. *Victorian Gardens.* Batsford, London 1986

Gallup, Barbara and Deborah Reich. *The Complete Book of Topiary.* Workman Publishing Co., New York 1987

Jellicoe, Geoffrey and Susan, Patrick Goode and Michael Lancaster. *The Oxford Companion to Gardens.* Oxford University Press, Oxford and New York 1986

Jones, Barbara. *Follies and Grottoes.* Constable and Co., London 1979

Lycett Green, Candida and Andrew Lawson. *Brilliant Gardens.* Chatto and Windus, London 1989

Maizels, John. *Raw Creation.* Phaidon Press, London 1996

Mazzanti, Anna (ed.). *Niki de Saint-Phalle – The Tarot Garden.* Edizioni Charta, Milan 1997

Mott, George. *Follies and Pleasure Pavilions.* Pavilion Books
in association with the National Trust, London 1989
Owen, Jane. *Eccentric Gardens.* Pavilion Books,
London 1990
Schuyt, Michael and Joost Elffers. *Fantastic Architecture.*
Thames and Hudson, London 1980

GARDENS CONTEMPORARY

Adams, William Howard. *Denatured Visions: Landscape and
Culture in the Twentieth Century.* Museum of Modern Art,
New York 1991
Adams, William Howard. *Roberto Burle Marx: The
Unnatural Art of the Garden.* Museum of Modern Art,
New York 1991
Beardsley, John. *Earthworks and Beyond: Contemporary Art in
the Landscape.* Abbeville Press, New York 1998
Celant, Germano. *Michael Heizer (Earthworks).* Fondazione
Prada, Italy 1997
Cooper, Guy and Gordon Taylor. *Gardens for the Future:
Gestures Against the Wild.* ConranOctopus, London 2000
Cooper, Guy and Gordon Taylor. *Mirrors of Paradise:
The Gardens of Fernando Caruncho.* The Monacelli Press,
New York 2000
Domaine de Kerguehennec, *Catalogue of Site Specific
Sculpture.* Brittany, France 1998
Eckbo, Garrett. *Garrett Eckbo: A Philosophy of Landscape.*
Process Architecture: No. 90, Tokyo 1990
Goldsworthy, Andy. *Touching North.* Fabian Carlsson,
Graeme Murray, London 1989
Goldsworthy, Andy. *Stone.* Viking Press, London 1994
Holden, Robert. *International Landscape Design.* Laurence
King Publishing, London 1996
Imbert, Dorothee. *The Modernist Garden in France.* Yale
University Press, 1993
Irwin, Robert. *Retrospective Exhibition: 1993.* Catalogue.
Museum of Contemporary Art, Los Angeles, California
Jellicoe, Geoffrey and Susan, Patrick Goode and Michael

Lancaster. *The Oxford Companion to Gardens.* Oxford
University Press, Oxford and New York 1986
Karson, Robin. *Fletcher Steele, Landscape Architect: An account
of a garden maker's life.* Abrams, New York 1989
Kiley, Dan and Jane Amidon. *Dan Kiley in His Own Words.*
Thames and Hudson, London 1999
Larsen, Jack Lenor. *A Weaver's Memoir.* Abrams Press,
New York 1998
Lund, Annemarie. *A Guide to Danish Landscape Architecture
1000–1996.* Arkitektens Forlag, Copenhagen 1997
Owen, Jane. *Unearthing the Seeds of Chaos Theory*
(Charles Jencks' Garden of Cosmological
Speculation in Scotland). *The Times Weekend.*
London, 6 December 1997
Pigeat, Jean-Paul. *Festival des Jardins* (Château de
Chaumont near Tours, France Annual International
Festival of Contemporary Gardens). Editions du
Chene-Hachette Livre, Paris 1995
Richardson, Tim. *How to Garden in a Jumping Universe.*
(Charles Jencks' Garden). *Country Life,* London,
23 October 1997
Richardson, Tim. Editor of *New Eden: The Contemporary
Gardens Magazine,* IPC. London 1999–2000
Spens, Michael. *Landscape Transformed.* Academy Editions,
London 1996
Spirn, Anne Whiston. *The Language of Landscape.* Yale
University Press, New Haven 1998
Treib, Marc and Dorothee Imbert. *Garrett Eckbo: Modern
Landscapes for Living.* University of California Press,
Berkeley and Los Angeles 1997
Treib, Marc. *Modern Landscape Architecture: A Critical Review.*
The MIT Press, Cambridge, Mass. 1998
Weilacher, Udo. *Between Landscape Architecture and Land Art.*
Birkhauser Publishing, Basel/Berlin/Boston 1996

Index